[IN THE KITCHEN WITH ANNA]

IN THE KITCHEN WITH ANNA

New Ways with the Classics

Anna Olson

whitecap

Whitecap Books is known for its expertise in the cookbook market, and has produced some
of the most innovative and familiar titles found in kitchens across North America. Visit our
website at www.whitecap.ca.

Edited by Grace Yaginuma
Proofread by Melva McLean
Design by Michelle Mayne
Photography by Ryan Szulc
Prop styling by Madeleine Johari
Food styling by Anna Olson

Printed in China

Library and Archives Canada Cataloguing in Publication

Olson, Anna, 1968–
    In the kitchen with Anna : new ways with the classics / Anna Olson.

Includes index.
ISBN 978-1-55285-946-9

    1. Cookery. I. Title.

TX715.6.O537 2008   641.5   C2008-903581-x

The publisher acknowledges the financial support of the Government of Canada through
the Book Publishing Industry Development Program (BPIDP) and the Province of British
Columbia through the Book Publishing Tax Credit.

09 10 11 12   5 4 3 2

Contents

ACKNOWLEDGMENTS

This book would be nothing but blank pages were it not for the names listed here. They are listed with heartfelt gratitude.

My husband, Michael, is my voice of reason (and humor), my mentor and my best friend. He has the innate ability to recognize when to listen, when to offer advice and when to offer a hug.

My parents, Andy and Donna, deserve to be sainted for their patience and their consistent respect while I (still) find my way. I grew up being allowed to make mistakes and be forgiven, and I appreciate that it is those very mistakes upon which I build and grow.

I hardly can believe that I have worked with Robert McCullough, my publisher, for almost ten years now, which is amazing since we are still only 27 years old! He is a dear friend, and I wish him happiness and contentment and that he continues to guide me.

My new friend, Grace Yaginuma, also deserves a humble nod as my editor. Her attention to detail, precision and grammatical resources are to be admired and revered. Through the magic of technology we have had long conversations through the body of this text, and while we haven't even shared a meal together, I feel I know her well. Grace: we must cook together sometime soon!

As you may have noticed, Ryan Szulc is a fantastic photographer, and it was a pleasure to host him and stylist Madeleine in my home as we took the photographs and then ate everything photographed.

The final credit goes to my army of recipe testers. They are friends (Lisa Rollo, I'll see you on set for some cheerleading), they are staff at Olson Foods, they are positive, caring people whom I value. While I can create and write and test recipes in my own kitchen, I find it indispensable to have other people test them and give me honest feedback. I thank each and every one of them for their part in this book. They include (in alphabetical order): Brittany Frees, Angela Greer, Madison Greer, John and Stacey Lazuruk, Sandi Moir, Trish Moscovitch, (Mrs.) Sue Sheldon, Gail Tufford, Stephanie Vail, Tracy Vencel-Krieger, Douglas Watt and Eric Wedderspoon.

INTRODUCTION

It's not likely you'll find me anywhere but in the kitchen most of the time. My kitchen is my sanctuary, my oasis. While cooking is my work, it is also my life, and it is rare that cooking ever feels like "work."

Cooking for me is grounding. When I look upon those dishes and meals that mean the most to me, they seem to be either a family recipe or something that recalls a specific memory of a time or place in my life—whether it was a meal shared with my husband, Michael, or with friends, or a recipe I acquired while working in New Orleans or Colorado many years ago. And I find myself trying to figure out exactly what element in the dish that takes me back. It's not just the taste of it, but sometimes the technique or even the texture.

For me, this personal connection is the value of a classic dish.

IF IT AIN'T BROKE . . .

Classic dishes are those that have stood the test of time: steak with Béarnaise, chicken Cordon Bleu, French onion soup are the first that pop into my mind. There's a reason these dishes have outlived others—they're delicious. A classic recipe has a distinct combination of flavors and/or features a certain cooking technique. I have great respect for the classics, which is why I have worked on this compilation with such fervor.

But sometimes the classics get lost in our daily shuffle of menu choices. Often the method is too time-intensive for our "I have 20 minutes to get supper ready"

schedules, or the grocery list is longer than our to-do list for the week, or perhaps the "old school" recipe is just too rich for our nutritionally sensitive palates.

All good things worth preserving can be improved upon, however. Those classic techniques and classic flavor combinations can be updated, while at the same time still respecting how they came about.

NEW WAYS WITH THE CLASSICS

Oh, I like the "old ways" too. In a professional restaurant kitchen, I'm more than happy to make lobster or shrimp bisque the old-fashioned way, by crushing the shells (which can be done in a giant industrial mixer!) to extract their flavor and proceed to make a giant mess. But in my home kitchen, my thinking and way of cooking changes. How can I make the same bisque without compromising flavor? (Check out the recipe on page 16 to find out how.)

The "new ways" involve looking for efficiencies within the recipe or within the contemporary kitchen itself. I am looking to simplify techniques, but only if it makes sense and does not compromise flavor. Often, I am sticking to classic flavor combinations but presenting it in a different, sometimes healthier format—my Chicken Cordon Bleu Panini (page 39) is a particular favorite. At the same time, there are a number of recipes I wish to share with you that are simply classics in my own repertoire. They may not have a history on fine dining restaurant menus, but they may be staples of mine, consistently made over the years.

RESPECT FOR THE CRAFT

I have learned so much from others as I write and share, and I recognize that discourse is vital to growing and finding "new ways" to cook.

One of the most important things I've learned is that cooking is essentially a *trade*. We have glamorized cooking to some extent, on television and in beautiful cookbooks, and I am happy with that since it has allowed me to share what I do with the world. But cooking is a craft, a trade—it can takes years of practice, and when you write the exam for chef's papers, you do it alongside other tradespeople like electricians and plumbers, who are required to fulfill an apprenticeship period before they can qualify themselves. I remind myself of this, and it keeps me humble. This business is not about self, it's about hospitality—in other words, serving and catering to others.

To be qualified means to respect techniques that work, and to practice them. Once I made the switch from savory cooking to baking, I found that my cooking improved because I had gained a deeper understanding of the science of what happens in the kitchen and the importance of technique. And getting to know the rules has also allowed me to bend and stretch them a bit, and understand when and where I can make changes and explain the "why" behind it.

ENJOY

In the end, what counts is that you enjoy the process of cooking as much as the end result. Regardless of whether you decide to master a new TECHNIQUE, try a new TASTE or read one of my TALES geared toward showing you my reason for loving the recipe, what I wish most is that you build your own culinary memory, making some of the dishes in this book your own new classics.

[SOUPS]

Good soup is not as simple as it seems. A brimming bowl of fragrant and flavorful liquid is actually quite an accomplishment. Often I judge the caliber of a restaurant not by its grilled beef tenderloin dish or delectable lobster salad, but by its soup du jour. A good soup can be concocted from the miscellaneous bits and pieces of produce and protein (a soup such as Canadian Minestrone on page 12 is a perfect example), but a truly special soup pays as much respect to the ingredients and method as roasting an expensive cut of beef. And this respect shows in the final result.

Many recipes utilize stock, most often chicken stock, as its liquid base. A good stock is as important an ingredient as the others. There are a number of good-quality chicken broth products on the market—most often in Tetra Paks, and most often organic. If sodium consumption is an issue for you, read the labels carefully. (Although the brand may be free of MSG, some are high in sodium.) A good chicken stock can be made easily, and without a formal recipe. Here's what I do. I take:

1 **whole chicken, cut into pieces**	2 **bay leaves**
2 **onions cut in half, peel intact**	2 **sprigs fresh thyme**
2 **celery stalks, roughly chopped**	5 **whole peppercorns**
2 **carrots, peeled or unpeeled and roughly chopped**	1 **sprig fresh parsley (optional)**

I plunk them all in a large stockpot and cover with cold water. I slowly bring it up to a gentle simmer over medium-low heat (no higher than medium). Once the fat and impurities start rising to the surface, skim the top of the stock with a spoon. Keep the stock at a bare simmer, uncovered, for 2½ hours from when it first starts to simmer—a vigorous boil would disturb the ingredients and the stock will come out cloudy. Strain the stock while it's still hot. Discard the veggies and herbs, and reserve the chicken meat for another use. It has had most of its flavor cooked out, but still has value, perfect for chicken salad or Chicken Cordon Bleu Panini (page 39).

When you have good stock, you can make great soup.

French Onion Soup 5

Chickpea, Chard & Potato Soup
    with Rosemary & Lemon 6

Chilled Beet Buttermilk Soup 7

Curried Lentil Soup with Spicy Cauliflower 8

Cream of Celery Soup with Blue Cheese 9

Auntie Annie's Chicken Noodle Soup 10

Canadian Minestrone 12

Vietnamese Beef Pho 14

Seafood Gumbo 15

Shrimp Bisque 16

FRENCH ONION SOUP

French onion soup has gone cliché, I think because it has slid off of fine dining menus and onto the blackboards of roadhouse restaurants. But it can be so good, an absolute favorite of mine to make at home. Caramelize the onions properly, use good stock and, of course, use good meltingly satisfying cheese on top, and you'll remember why it became so popular in the first place.

Over medium heat, heat the oil and butter in a large heavy-bottomed soup pot (see Technique). Add the onions and cook down, stirring often, until caramelized—be patient, this takes about 45 minutes.

Add the garlic and thyme and cook for 1 minute. Add the sherry and stir with a wooden spoon, gently pulling up any caramelized bits from the bottom of the pot. Add the stock and bring to a boil, then lower the heat and simmer gently for about 20 minutes. Season to taste.

Preheat the oven to broil. Place 6 ovenproof bowls (or mugs) on a baking sheet and ladle in the hot soup. Place a toasted baguette slice on each and top each with ⅓ cup (80 mL) of grated cheese. Broil until the cheese is melted and bubbling, and serve. (Be careful—it's hot!)

Serves 6

2 Tbsp **olive oil** 30 mL
2 Tbsp **butter** 30 mL
8 cups **sliced onions** 2 L
2 cloves **garlic, minced**
2 tsp **chopped fresh thyme** 10 mL
¼ cup **dry sherry** 60 mL
5 cups **beef or chicken stock** 1.25 L
salt & pepper
6 slices **day-old baguette (white or whole wheat), lightly toasted**
2 cups **grated Gruyère or Emmenthal cheese** 500 mL

TASTE I love sherry and caramelized onions together, both in the pot and at the table. I prefer a sherry with just a hint of sweetness, such as an Amontillado. The same sherry pairs well with the Gruyère or Emmenthal cheese, which have a beautiful nuttiness to them.

TECHNIQUE Success lies in caramelizing those onions. I prefer to use a cast iron enamel pot or a heavy-bottomed stainless steel pot as opposed to a nonstick pot. About halfway through cooking, once a lot of the moisture has evaporated from the onions, the sugars will start to caramelize and stick to the bottom of the pot. A gentle stir with a wooden spoon coaxes them from sticking too much, and once the sherry and stock have been added, the bottom of the pot will be clean, with all the flavor and color now worked into the broth.

TALE I know you'll think that 8 cups seems like too many onions, and then, once the onions cook down to a quarter of their volume, you'll think it was not enough! (The caramelized onions plump up once you add the stock and essentially rehydrate themselves.) Too often I've forgotten this, believing I need even more than 8 cups, only to end up with an onion stew . . .

CHICKPEA, CHARD & POTATO SOUP WITH ROSEMARY & LEMON
This soup has Spanish-inspired roots for me, but if you've ever had its Portuguese counterpart, *caldo verde*, it might seem familiar to you.

Heat the olive oil in a soup pot over medium heat. Sauté the onion until translucent, about 5 minutes. Add the garlic, lemon zest and rosemary and stir for a minute (see Technique). Add the chicken stock and potatoes, cover the pot loosely and bring to a simmer. Lower the heat and simmer until the potatoes are tender, about 20 minutes. Stir in the chickpeas.

Wash the Swiss chard and separate the stems from the leaves. Chop the stems into 1-inch (2.5 cm) pieces and add to the soup, simmering for 5 minutes. Roughly chop the leaves and add to the soup, now leaving the pot uncovered and simmering just until the chard has wilted, about 3 minutes. Season to taste.

Immediately before serving stir in the lemon juice. Top soup bowls with chopped parsley. *Serves 6*

2 Tbsp **olive oil** 30 mL
1 cup **diced onion** 250 mL
2 cloves **garlic, minced**
2 tsp **finely grated lemon zest** 10 mL
2 tsp **finely chopped fresh rosemary** 10 mL
5 cups **chicken stock** 1.25 L
6 **sliced white mini potatoes**
1 can **(14 oz/398 mL) chickpeas, drained and rinsed**
½ bunch **Swiss chard**
salt & pepper
2 Tbsp **lemon juice** 30 mL
3 Tbsp **chopped fresh Italian parsley, for garnish** 45 mL

TASTE This is a hearty soup without being heavy. The broth is fragrant with lemon and rosemary, while the chickpeas, iron-rich chard and potatoes add body. Using a good vegetable stock would make this a tasty vegetarian option.

TECHNIQUE Sautéing the rosemary for a minute before adding the liquid really draws out the flavor. Two teaspoons of rosemary may not seem like a lot, but it is one of those herbs that keeps getting bigger in flavor as it sits in its dish.

TALE I first had this soup in Spain, as a guest on a pig and cork farm—a farm that raised pigs and grew trees for wine corks. Yes, it sounds like a strange combination, but the hilly farm estate was covered with oak trees. The cork was harvested from the trees, and the very same trees provided shade and, more importantly, acorns for the free-running Iberian black-footed pig, which is the main component of the internationally known *jamón ibérico*—a Spanish version of prosciutto that tastes nutty.

CHILLED BEET BUTTERMILK SOUP

This chilled soup is a vibrant fuchsia color, and garnishing it with a beet sorbet keeps it refreshing. I have even served it in vintage tea cups. Be careful, though—you don't want to wear a white shirt if you're inclined to drip.

Bring the chicken stock, beets, onion, carrot, garlic, lemon juice and sugar in a soup pot up to a simmer over medium heat. Cook until the beets are tender, about 40 minutes. Purée using a blender, food processor or immersion blender until smooth. Strain through a sieve and cool to room temperature. Whisk in the buttermilk and season. Stir in dill. Chill at least 4 hours before serving. Check the seasoning, as the soup may need more salt and pepper.

Garnish with sour cream and/or beet sorbet. *Serves 6*

BEET SORBET
½ lb **beets, cooked, peeled and diced** 250 g
2 cups **white wine** 500 mL
2 Tbsp **sugar** 30 mL
½ tsp **fine salt** 2 mL
1 **egg white**

Purée all the ingredients until smooth. Pour into an ice cream maker and make the sorbet following manufacturer's instructions. Scrape sorbet into a separate container and put it in the freezer until it's completely firm (the sorbet will be too soft to serve directly from the ice cream maker). *Makes about 2 cups (500 mL)*

4 cups **chicken stock** 1 L
1 lb **fresh beets, peeled and diced** 500 g
1 cup **diced onion** 250 mL
¾ cup **peeled and diced carrot** 190 mL
1 clove **garlic, minced**
1 Tbsp **lemon juice** 15 mL
1 tsp **sugar** 5 mL
1½ cups **buttermilk** 375 mL
salt & pepper
2 Tbsp **chopped fresh dill** 30 mL
sour cream, for garnish
Beet Sorbet, for garnish

TASTE A perfect balance of flavors is achieved very simply by pairing beets, which are naturally sweet, with tangy buttermilk, which makes the soup taste creamy and rich. But as buttermilk only has 1 to 3.5% milk fat, the soup is actually quite lean.

TECHNIQUE Be sure that your beet mixture is completely cooled before adding the buttermilk. Buttermilk curdles when heated, so you definitely do not want to serve this warm.

TALE I first saw a beet sorbet when I worked as an apprentice in Vail, Colorado. A sweeter version of this was served with a warm chocolate cake, and I was amazed and impressed by the combination. Add ⅓ cup (80 mL) more sugar to this recipe and you've got yourself a dessert sorbet.

CURRIED LENTIL SOUP WITH SPICY CAULIFLOWER

This soup definitely fulfills its goal aromatic-wise. The cauliflower still has crunch to it, so it makes a nice contrast in texture and taste with the soup. Also a good contrast is adding hot sauce only to the cauliflower and not to the soup.

2 Tbsp **olive oil** 30 mL
⅔ cup **finely diced onion** 160 mL
1 cup **finely diced carrot** 250 mL
2 cloves **garlic, minced**
1 Tbsp **finely minced ginger** 15 mL
1 Tbsp **ground cumin** 15 mL
1 Tbsp **ground coriander** 15 mL

2 tsp **ground turmeric** 10 mL
¼ tsp **ground cloves** 1 mL
1½ cups **green lentils (not French or du Puy), rinsed** 375 mL
5 cups **chicken or vegetable stock** 1.25 L
1 cup **diced tomato, fresh or canned** 250 mL
salt & pepper

Heat the olive oil in a soup pot over medium heat. Add the onion and carrots and sauté until carrots have softened a little, about 5 minutes. Stir in the garlic, ginger and spices and cook for 1 minute. Add the lentils and chicken stock, and bring to a gentle simmer. Loosely cover the pot and continue simmering for about 30 minutes, stirring occasionally until the lentils are tender. Stir in the tomato and cook for 10 minutes more. Season to taste.

Stir the soup before ladling into bowls so that enough lentils are in each bowl. Garnish with Spicy Cauliflower (recipe below). *Serves 6*

SPICY CAULIFLOWER
2 Tbsp **olive oil** 30 mL
⅓ head **fresh cauliflower, cut into very small florets**
salt & pepper
splash **hot sauce, such as Sriracha**

Heat the olive oil in a sauté pan over medium-high heat. Add the cauliflower florets and a dash of salt and pepper. Toss the cauliflower occasionally, but let it brown a little bit, cooking for about 4 minutes. Add ½ cup (125 mL) of water and hot sauce and cover the pan immediately. Boil for 4 minutes, then uncover and continue to cook until water evaporates. Adjust the seasoning, and serve warm on soup. *Makes about 2 cups (500 mL)*

TASTE I love the earthiness of green lentils, but I have made the same soup a little lighter in taste and texture by making it with red lentils instead. And I cannot profess to be an expert in Indian cooking, but you could say that the combination of garlic and ginger along with this assortment of spices is kind of like my own garam masala.

TECHNIQUE When making the Spicy Cauliflower, browning it on the outside actually lends almost a smoky taste to the cauliflower, which I love—so much so that I like to use more than just an average "garnish" portion. The soup then becomes more of a meal.

TALE I often make this soup when I need to get out of a cooking or eating rut. We all fall into routine, and filling the house with heady aromatics can remind me to "wake up and smell the spices" and inspire me to get creative in the kitchen again.

CREAM OF CELERY SOUP WITH BLUE CHEESE

It's all about the joy of simplicity here. Just when you thought you had nothing in the fridge and were about to dial for a pizza, you realize that the celery in the crisper—usually that last veggie on the crudité platter, or the behind-the-scenes flavor builder for other dishes—can actually be the superstar in a pot of soup. Even a recipe ingredient deserves its 15 minutes of fame.

3 Tbsp **butter** 45 mL
1 cup **diced onion** 250 mL
3 cups **diced celery (½-inch/1 cm dice)** 750 mL
3 Tbsp **all-purpose flour** 45 mL
3 cups **2% milk** 750 mL
2 cups **chicken stock** 500 mL

1 Tbsp **chopped fresh thyme** 15 mL
1 **bay leaf**
2 Tbsp **dry vermouth** 30 mL
salt & pepper
3 oz **blue cheese, crumbled** 90 g
2 Tbsp **chopped fresh chives** 30 mL

Melt the butter in a soup pot over medium heat. Sauté the onion and celery until the onion is translucent, about 5 minutes. Sift in the flour and stir with a wooden spoon, cooking for 4 minutes. Add ½ cup (125 mL) milk and stir vigorously to create a paste. Switch to a whisk add the remaining milk, 1 cup (250 mL) at a time, whisking constantly. Whisk in the chicken stock, thyme and bay leaf and bring to a simmer. Lower the heat, cover loosely, and simmer for 10 minutes or until the celery is tender. Remove the bay leaf and stir in the vermouth. Season to taste.

Serve soup topped with the crumbled blue cheese and chopped chives. *Serves 6*

TASTE If you grow lovage in your garden, add a few chopped leaves to the soup to heighten the celery flavor. I actually really enjoy the taste of celery, but like many I take it for granted.

TECHNIQUE This classic soup preparation is called a *velouté*, which literally means "velvety"—and this soup does have a velvety texture. I think it's fabulous that you don't necessarily have to add cream to make a soup taste creamy.

TALE I had a roommate in university who lived on canned cream of celery soup and toasted bagels—she had it at least three times a week! If only I'd known how to make a velouté then, I could have made a tastier version for her.

AUNTIE ANNIE'S CHICKEN NOODLE SOUP

There's chicken noodle soup and then there's *chicken noodle soup*. Like any good soup made by a relative, preferably at least a generation older than you, chicken noodle soup has that magical power to heal, soothe and strengthen. This recipe even includes homemade soup noodles. Making the chicken stock from scratch is essential—Grandma called it "first cook," and then the making of the actual soup "second cook."

8 cups **homemade chicken stock (see page 3), reserving 1 Tbsp (15 mL) of the chicken fat (see below)** 2 L

1 cup **finely diced onion** 250 mL

1 cup **finely diced celery** 250 mL

1 cup **finely diced carrot** 250 mL

1 cup **peeled and diced rutabaga or kohlrabi** 250 mL

1 tsp **chopped fresh thyme** 5 mL

½ tsp **Hungarian paprika** 2 mL

2 **boneless skinless chicken breasts, diced**

1 recipe **Egg Noodles (see facing page)**

salt & pepper

chopped fresh parsley, for garnish

Make the chicken stock but reserve some of the chicken fat as it rises to the surface, being careful not to collect any of the impurities. Alternately, the chicken stock can be prepared a day ahead, and the fat easily removed once chilled. (Use the chicken meat for another occasion; this soup will use fresh chicken meat.)

In a large soup pot, add the 1 Tbsp (15 mL) of reserved chicken fat. Over medium heat, sauté the onion, celery, carrot and rutabaga (or kohlrabi) until the onions are translucent, about 5 minutes. Add the thyme, paprika, diced chicken and chicken stock to the pot. Bring up to a simmer and cook, uncovered, until the vegetables are tender and the chicken is cooked.

To serve, prepare and cook the egg noodles following the recipe below and place a generous spoonful of freshly cooked noodles into each bowl. Garnish with fresh parsley and serve. *Serves 8*

EGG NOODLES

1 cup **all-purpose flour** 250 mL
2 **large eggs**
1 tsp **fine salt** 5 mL

Sift the flour onto a clean work surface (counter or large wooden cutting board), and make a well in the center. Break the eggs into the well and add the salt. With a spoon or with the tips of your fingers stir the broken eggs in circular motions, bringing in a bit of flour at a time. Once all the flour is incorporated, knead the dough until very smooth, about 5 minutes. Sprinkle the work surface and the top of dough with a little flour and cover with a tea towel. Let the dough rest for 30 minutes.

Cut the dough into two pieces and roll out one half of the dough as thinly as possible, lifting the dough at the edges and shaking it from time to time to ensure it is not sticking. Sprinkle the dough with a little flour then roll it up into a spiral. Slice the noodles as thinly as possible and spread out onto the work surface to dry for 20 minutes. Repeat with the second half.

Noodles can be blanched in salted boiling water for 2 minutes and then used, or frozen until ready to cook.

TASTE You can't beat real homemade chicken soup. The two steps of making it—first the broth, and then the soup—are essential, and the old rule does follow: soup always tastes better the second day. So get that pot on the stove when you first feel that tickle of a cold coming on—you'll want the soup for tomorrow.

TECHNIQUE Rolling up the dough and then slicing ensures that the noodles are consistently thin. I don't know what my Great Auntie Annie did, but I heard her noodles always looked perfect.

TALE Aunt Andrea claims I inherited my gift for cooking from Great Auntie Annie, whom I only met when I was an infant. She was a caterer in Cleveland, Ohio, and would cater Slovak weddings at her church hall for up to 500 people. The legend goes that if she really liked the bride and groom, she would make them her special homemade noodles when she made the soup.

CANADIAN MINESTRONE

Minestrone is the Italian vegetable soup, but add peameal bacon and a hint of maple syrup and you've got a new classic.

6 slices **regular bacon, diced**
⅔ cup **diced onion** 160 mL
⅔ cup **peeled and diced carrot (½-inch/1 cm dice)** 160 mL
½ cup **peeled and diced parsnip (½-inch/1 cm dice)** 125 mL
⅔ cup **diced green zucchini (½-inch/1 cm dice)** 160 mL
⅔ cup **diced red bell pepper (½-inch/1 cm dice)** 160 mL
2 cloves **garlic, minced**
2 tsp **chopped fresh thyme** 10 mL
1 **bay leaf**

1 can **(14 oz/398 mL) white kidney beans, drained and rinsed**
1 can **(14 oz/398 mL) diced tomato**
3 cups **chicken stock** 750 mL
2 Tbsp **maple syrup** 30 mL
salt & pepper
about 1 cup **dried soup pasta, such as orzo or** *acini di pepe* **("peppercorn" pasta)** about 250 mL
12 slices **peameal bacon**
½ cup **finely grated Parmesan cheese** 125 mL
¼ cup **finely chopped fresh Italian parsley** 60 mL

Cook the bacon over medium heat in a large soup pot until crisp. Remove the bacon from the pot and set aside. Add the onion, carrot and parsnip to the bacon fat and sauté 5 minutes. Add the zucchini, red pepper, garlic, thyme and bay leaf and sauté 1 minute more. Add the kidney beans, tomato, chicken stock and maple syrup. Cover loosely and simmer until the vegetables are tender, about 20 minutes. Remove the bay leaf and season to taste.

While the soup is simmering, cook the pasta in boiling salted water until just tender, then drain and rinse to halt cooking. Set aside. Cook the peameal slices in a sauté pan over medium-high heat, about 5 minutes on each side until cooked through. Slice it into bite-sized strips.

To serve, rinse cooked pasta again but using hot water to warm it, then drain. Spoon a few tablespoons of pasta into each soup dish, then ladle soup on top. Sprinkle each soup dish with strips of peameal bacon, the reserved bacon bits, Parmesan and parsley. *Serves 6*

TASTE This is one of those recipes you can easily personalize. By looking into your own fridge, you probably spy your own favorite ingredients. Perhaps you buy turnip and green pepper more often than parsnip and red pepper—well, that works just fine. And you always have black beans in your pantry, not white kidney beans? Go ahead and use them instead.

TECHNIQUE What counts in any soup that has "bits" in it is that the pieces of vegetable are all cut to as close to the same size as possible, and that a few vegetable pieces fit easily onto your spoon. (All culinary students are graded on this in their first year of cooking school.)

TALE How did I come up with this version of minestrone soup? Leftovers, of course. I wanted to use up some peameal bacon I had from a Sunday breakfast, and, like magic, a new personality to minestrone emerged.

VIETNAMESE BEEF PHO

Pho is believed to be the Vietnamese interpretation of the French "pot au feu," a broth-cooked stew of meat and vegetables. The Asian version is rich in fragrance and has a fresh kick to it in that some of the elements are added at the table right before eating.

FOR THE BROTH

1 **large onion, peeled and cut in half**
1 inch **fresh ginger, sliced** 2.5 cm
3 **whole cloves**
1 **whole star anise**
1 **small cinnamon stick**
8 cups **beef stock, home-made or store-bought** 2 L

FOR ASSEMBLY

2 cups **bean sprouts** 500 mL
½ cup **fresh basil leaves (preferably Thai basil)** 125 mL
1 **lime, quartered**
8 oz **(dried) vermicelli rice noodles, cooked following package instructions** 240 g
12 oz **raw beef flank steak (also called "London broil"), thinly sliced** 375 g
hoisin sauce
Sriracha sauce

For the broth, heat a heavy-bottomed soup pot over high heat. (No oil is necessary.) Sear or scorch the onion flat side down until dark brown, and then turning occasionally until all sides have browned, about 3 minutes. Add the ginger, spices and beef stock and bring up to a simmer. Simmer, loosely covered, for 15 minutes. Strain and return broth to a simmer.

While the soup is simmering, divide bean sprouts, basil and lime quarters onto 4 plates.

To assemble, warm up the cooked rice noodles by immersing them in a pot of simmering water or the broth. Place about 1 cup (250 mL) of the hot rice noodles in each serving bowl. Arrange slices of beef flank over the noodles, and ladle 2 cups (500 mL) of simmering broth into each bowl, pouring over the beef. Let everyone garnish their own soup with the bean sprouts, basil (torn into the bowl), lime juice, hoisin and Sriracha. (Watch out—the Sriracha gets really hot by the time you reach the bottom of the bowl!) *Serves 4*

TASTE Like all good soup, the broth makes it, and the combination of spices yields that distinctive aroma to a well-made *pho*. I like that you can add as much or as little hot sauce as you wish, along with the amount of bean sprouts, basil, lime and hoisin, since everyone at the table is customizing his or her own bowl. Thai basil has a subtle licorice note to it, but regular basil works just fine.

TECHNIQUE Searing the onion for soup was new to me—I'm accustomed to either sweating onions to avoid color, or slowly caramelizing them. But for this soup, searing the onion in the pot adds a little smoky taste to the broth (and any slight scorching in the pot is lifted away by the liquid).

TALE Both Michael and I learned how to cook pho from our friend Hung Vo, who owns a great Vietnamese restaurant called Mai Vi in St. Catharines, Ontario. He was so open with us in demystifying cooking techniques so different from North American and European techniques. Pho is a classic in its own right.

SEAFOOD GUMBO

Never had okra before? This is the best way to try it for the first time. This soup is so packed with veggies and shrimp that it is more like a stew.

ROUX

¼ cup **vegetable oil** 60 mL
⅓ cup **all-purpose flour** 80 mL

GUMBO

2 Tbsp **vegetable oil** 30 mL
1 cup **finely diced onion** 250 mL
1 cup **finely diced celery** 250 mL
1 cup **finely diced green pepper** 250 mL
3 cloves **garlic, minced**
1 **jalapeño, seeded and minced**
1 Tbsp **chopped fresh oregano** 15 mL
4 cups **chicken stock** 1 L
1 cup **diced tomato, fresh or canned** 250 mL
pinch **celery salt**
6 oz **crabmeat (tinned or frozen)** 175 g
1½ cups **fresh or frozen okra, stems removed and chopped** 375 mL
8 oz **small shrimp (51/60), peeled and deveined and tails removed** 240 g
salt & pepper
4 cups **freshly cooked long-grain rice** 1 L

For the roux, stir ¼ cup (60 mL) of oil and the flour in a small saucepan over medium heat. Cook the roux until it turns a rich caramel color, stirring constantly with a wooden spoon. After about 20 minutes it will have the texture of peanut butter, but should be a touch darker (see Technique). If the roux seems to be browning at the bottom of the pan too quickly, reduce the heat. Set aside.

For the gumbo, heat the 2 Tbsp (30 mL) oil in a large soup pot over medium heat. Add the onion, celery and pepper and sauté for 3 minutes. Add the garlic, jalapeño and oregano, stirring for 1 minute. Stir in the roux to coat the vegetables. Gradually whisk in the chicken stock, then add the tomato and celery salt and bring up to a simmer, still over medium heat. Add the crabmeat and okra and simmer, partly covered, until the okra is tender, about 15 minutes. Stir in the shrimp and cook just until the shrimp turns pink. Season to taste and serve immediately in large bowls over rice. *Serves 8*

TASTE There are particular elements that qualify a gumbo: the okra (not only for its taste but also as thickening), seafood and/or sausage, a dark roux and the "holy trinity" of onion, celery and green pepper.

TECHNIQUE The effort of a good gumbo is all in the roux (the flour and oil mixture). I make the roux and let it slowly brown while I am preparing all the other ingredients, but right next to the stove so I can closely watch it. The moment you think it's done, let it go another two minutes—the darker the better!

TALE I worked for a short while at a restaurant in the French Quarter in New Orleans. We sold so much gumbo that making the roux was a full-day process in itself. Every week, we would pour 8 quarts (or *liters*, in Canadian) of oil into two large pans and stir in about 12 pounds of flour. This mess would go into the oven, and we would cook it all day, stirring it every hour as it slowly darkened. And this would only last us a week. That's a lot of gumbo.

SHRIMP BISQUE

With the price of shrimp almost the same price as chicken these days, shrimp bisque needn't be a soup relegated to holiday occasions, nor be so difficult to make that you need to take a vacation day off work to make it.

Peel and devein the shrimp, reserving the shells. Melt 2 Tbsp (30 mL) butter in a large pot over medium heat. Add the shrimp shells and cook until they're fully pink in color. Add the Pernod and reduce the liquid by half. Add 8 cups (2 L) of water, lemon halves and bay leaf and slowly bring to a simmer (still over medium heat—see Technique), and continue simmering the stock for 30 minutes. Strain through a fine strainer and set aside the stock.

In a large soup pot, melt the remaining 2 Tbsp (30 mL) butter over medium heat. Add the shrimp and sauté until pink, about 5 minutes. Remove from the soup pot and set aside. Add the onion, celery, red pepper, fennel and carrot and sauté until the onions are translucent, about 5 minutes. Add the rice, tomato paste and shrimp stock. Return to the heat and bring to a simmer. Add the cayenne, nutmeg and salt and cook until the vegetables and rice are tender, about 25 minutes. Add the cream and all but ½ cup (125 mL) of the shrimp. Let the soup cool down a bit, and purée in a food processor or blender. (If using a blender, vent the lid and cover with a towel.) Strain the soup, return to a low heat and adjust seasoning to taste.

For garnish, finely chop the reserved ½ cup (125 mL) shrimp and sprinkle on top of the bisque along with the reserved ½ cup (125 mL) of diced fennel. *Serves 8*

4 Tbsp **butter, divided** 60 mL
2 lb **shrimp (31/40)** 1 kg
½ cup **Pernod** 125 mL
1 **lemon, cut in half**
1 **bay leaf**
1 **medium onion, chopped**
2 **celery stalks, chopped**
1 **red bell pepper, seeded and diced**
1 cup **chopped fresh fennel bulb, plus** ½ cup (125 mL) **finely diced for garnish** 250 mL
1 cup **peeled and diced carrot** 250 mL
2 Tbsp **uncooked long-grain rice** 30 mL
2 Tbsp **tomato paste** 30 mL
½ tsp **cayenne pepper** 2 mL
¼ tsp **ground nutmeg** 1 mL
salt, to season
½ cup **whipping cream (35%)** 125 mL

TASTE Pernod and tomato are the distinctive background flavors of a good seafood bisque, whether it's shrimp, crab or lobster. And the fennel in this recipe adds body and highlights the elegant yet subtle licorice notes of Pernod.

TECHNIQUE Cooking the shrimp shells and making a stock from them is the traditional method for making a bisque. The shells are laden with flavor, but it only takes half an hour to extract their worth. Bringing the stock to a simmer gradually over moderate heat ensures a clear stock—the impurities will rise slowly to the surface, which you should remove with a spoon.

TALE Until recently, I was daunted by making bisque at home, only because of the scale of production I remember in restaurant kitchens. When making lobster bisque, we used to put dozens of cleaned lobster shells in a large, 40-quart stand mixer that would crush the shells to smithereens and extract every bit of flavor. It was a noisy, messy job (with delicious results!), and it took me a while to figure out that making bisque doesn't have to be such a huge enterprise.

[SALADS]

A good salad is the ultimate paradox—it should be inherently complex in color, in texture and in taste, but it should also be remarkably simple. A good salad should not be so complicated in its flavor blending or in its preparation that it masks those very elements that should stand out. So how is this achieved?

Seasonality is the first key to a successful salad. A tomato salad in January not only is a pale shadow of what could be made in August, but the tomatoes cost three times as much. Pick ingredients that are at their best at that moment. And so often I say—to the point of sounding like a broken record (or scratched CD for those born after 1975…) —*what grows together goes together*. Fresh, ripe tomatoes with fresh basil—is there anything better?

Second is balance. I look at a good salad as a perfect tease of all the taste and texture sensors on our palate. A good salad should have—

• crunch—from crisp greens, nuts, seeds, croutons
• tartness—from vinegar, citrus, even tomatoes
• creaminess—from cheese, olive oil, avocado
• saltiness—not only from finishing salts, but from cheese, salted nuts
• a subtle sweetness—from fruit, honey, tomatoes

No wonder tomatoes appear in salads so much—they can act as more than one important element of a good salad.

I use salad to start a meal, to cleanse the palate after a rich meal, as a side to grilled items or as a meal itself. It's all good, so long as it's all fresh.

Heirloom Tomatoes with Herbed
    Ricotta 21
Arugula with Avocado, Blackberry
    & Feta 22
Bitter Greens with Tender Fruits
    & Chèvre 24
Spinach, Beet & Orange Salad 25
Contemporary Cobb Salad 26
Deconstructed Waldorf Salad 29
Celery Root, Apple & Onion Slaw 30
Cucumber Three Ways 31
Turkey Salad with Dried Apricot
    & Marjoram 32
Five-Bean Salad 33

HEIRLOOM TOMATOES WITH HERBED RICOTTA

I do love tomatoes, and the light creaminess of ricotta is a perfect companion for the varying tastes and textures of different tomato varieties. (The herbed ricotta is also delicious atop pizza, spread onto crostini or even as a dip.) Should heirlooms not be an option, a good, ripe beefsteak tomato from the farmers' market is equally satisfying.

1½ cups **soft ricotta cheese** 375 mL

1 Tbsp **chopped fresh chives** 15 mL

1 Tbsp **chopped fresh basil** 15 mL

1 Tbsp **chopped fresh mint** 15 mL

coarse salt & pepper

1½ lb **heirloom and/or multi-color tomatoes** 750 g

good quality extra virgin olive oil

Stir the ricotta with the chives, basil and mint and season to taste.

Slice the tomatoes (see Technique) and arrange on a salad plate. Spoon dollops of ricotta over the tomatoes, drizzle lightly with olive oil and sprinkle with more salt and pepper. *Serves 6*

TASTE Typically yellow and orange tomatoes taste sweeter because they have lower acidity, but if searching out heirloom varieties, prepare to be surprised. What may look like an under-ripe speckled green tomato can turn out to be wonderfully sweet, and a deeply colored Bull's Blood tomato may actually be quite mild.

TECHNIQUE There is an art to slicing tomatoes. A sharp knife is essential—it can even have a slightly serrated edge to it. You want to be able to cut through the skin without crushing the delicate interior of a ripe tomato. Slice as thinly as you can, depending on how juicy the tomato is.

TALE Michael and I served this salad to Queen Elizabeth's royal entourage many years ago. We called it "Painter's Palette of Tomatoes," and I remember peeking into the dining room of the restaurant and being impressed by how the colorful plates dressed up the room.

ARUGULA WITH AVOCADO, BLACKBERRY & FETA

Sometimes simplest is best. Composing this salad is easy—but take the time to appreciate the complexity of the flavor combinations.

2 bunches **(about 6 cups/ 1.5 L) arugula, washed and trimmed**

1 **ripe avocado**

½ pint **fresh blackberries** 250 mL

½ cup **crumbled feta cheese** 125 mL

juice of 1 lime

good quality extra virgin olive oil

salt & pepper

Arrange the arugula onto salad plates. Cut the avocado in half and peel. Slice and arrange the avocado over the greens. Wash the blackberries and sprinkle over. Top with feta cheese. Sprinkle salad with lime juice and olive oil and season lightly with salt and pepper. *Serves 6*

TASTE Fresh blackberries can be like a refreshing drink of water nestled within a salad, and the way they play against the creaminess of ripe avocado is magic.

TECHNIQUE When you've got all the main flavor elements you need within the body of a salad, then you don't need a complicated vinaigrette. Just a sprinkle of lime juice and a touch of good quality extra virgin olive oil ties the whole salad together seamlessly.

TALE I made this salad for a cooking class recently and served it alongside slices of grilled New York steak. Within a week I had many of the students come back to tell me they made this salad and steak at home. I love to impress with simplicity!

BITTER GREENS WITH TENDER FRUITS & CHÈVRE

This salad is a fabulous companion to grilled fish or seafood. A simple skewer of shrimp marinated in lemon juice and fresh cilantro would complement the salad perfectly.

6 cups **bitter greens such as arugula, radicchio and Belgian endive** 1.5 L
1 **green onion**
1 **ripe nectarine**
2 **fresh apricots**
½ lb **fresh sweet cherries** 250 g
1 Tbsp **chopped fresh cilantro** 15 mL

1 tsp **finely grated lemon zest** 5 mL
1 Tbsp **lemon juice** 15 mL
pinch ground cinnamon
3 oz **fresh chèvre** 90 g
good quality extra virgin olive oil
salt & pepper

Arrange the bitter greens on a serving platter. Chop the green onion and sprinkle over the greens.

Thinly slice the nectarine (with skin on) and place in a small bowl. Cut the apricots in half, remove the pits and slice thinly. Pit the cherries and cut in half. Toss the fruits with fresh cilantro, lemon zest, lemon juice and cinnamon. Spoon the fruit over the salad greens, and crumble the pieces of chèvre on top. Drizzle the salad with olive oil and season lightly. Serve immediately. *Serves 6*

TASTE *Tender fruit* is a term that refers to any fruit that grows with a pit. Apricots are my personal favorite. Their peak season in July is so short, and they are so delicate that you have to eat them right away, so I absolutely obsess over them for the two weeks they are at their finest.

TECHNIQUE This salad can be equally appreciated in winter if you freeze any tender fruits. While the texture of the fruit will be much softer, their robust, peak-season flavor is preserved, and the marinade will further awaken the fruits' summery characteristics. A great trick for nectarines as well as peaches is to freeze them whole, skins intact—the skin is nature's best plastic wrap. When thawed, the skin peels right off and you have a relatively firm juicy fruit.

TALE Michael and I are addicted to arugula. We love to eat it as a "finishing salad," served after our main course to cleanse the palate.

SPINACH, BEET & ORANGE SALAD

This salad suits any season, but I like it best in the fall, when beets are sweet and citrus is coming into its peak season. If in season, try blood oranges in this salad. They have an intensity that works beautifully against the sweet beets.

To cook the beets, preheat the oven to 375°F (190°C). Peel the beets with a vegetable peeler, cut into small wedges, toss with a touch of olive oil and season lightly (see Technique). Roast, covered tightly, until fork-tender, about 25 minutes. Let cool, but do not chill in the refrigerator. (You may do so if preparing this in advance, but let the beets come to room temperature before serving.)

Peel the oranges with a knife, removing all the pith. Segment oranges between the membranes with a paring knife, over a bowl to catch any excess orange juices. Reserve the orange segments. Whisk the orange juice with lemon juice, chives, tarragon and mustard. Gradually whisk in the olive oil until incorporated and season to taste.

To assemble, spread the spinach greens onto a serving platter and arrange the beets and orange segments on top. Spoon over the dressing and serve. *Serves 6*

1 lb **fresh small beets** 500 g
olive oil, for roasting
coarse salt & pepper
2 **navel oranges**
2 tsp **lemon juice** 10 mL
1 Tbsp **chopped fresh chives** 15 mL
1 tsp **chopped fresh tarragon** 5 mL
¼ tsp **Dijon mustard** 1 mL
2 Tbsp **olive oil** 30 mL
more **coarse salt & pepper**
6 cups **spinach greens, stems trimmed** 1.5 L

TASTE A little tarragon finds a perfect home in so many salads. Its delicate licorice nuance heightens other flavors without being overpowering.

TECHNIQUE Beets peel easily with a vegetable peeler. And if they are cut up and roasted, they are ready in a fraction of the time it takes to boil them whole. Oven roasting also concentrates the sweetness and mineral characteristics of beets.

TALE I've tried to make it a policy never to serve a gritty salad. When I have company over, I always wash and spin the spinach at least three times. Okay, when it's just the two of us at home, I probably only wash and spin twice, but only after I've tasted a leaf to be sure it's clean.

CONTEMPORARY COBB SALAD

This salad is definitely a meal. The original Cobb salad was created by the owner of the Brown Derby restaurant in Los Angeles decades ago. I have worked in all the usual ingredients of the salad, but with a twist. Instead of each ingredient laid individually on top of the greens side by side, I've created three distinct salads to be served together.

CHICKEN SALAD

2 cups **diced cooked chicken meat** 500 mL
⅓ cup **chopped green onion** 80 mL
¼ cup **mayonnaise** 60 mL
1 Tbsp **red wine vinegar** 15 mL
3 oz **blue cheese** 90 g
salt & pepper

EGG & BACON SALAD

1 Tbsp **red wine vinegar** 15 mL
1 Tbsp **chopped fresh chives** 15 mL
½ tsp **Dijon mustard** 2 mL
3 Tbsp **olive oil** 45 mL
salt & pepper
4 **hard-boiled eggs, peeled**
4 **strips bacon, cooked and diced**

TOMATO AVOCADO SALAD

1 **ripe avocado, peeled and diced**
1 pint **grape tomatoes, cut in half** 500 mL
½ cup **finely diced red onion** 125 mL
1 tsp **finely grated lime zest** 5 mL
1 Tbsp **olive oil** 15 mL
2 tsp **fresh lime juice** 10 mL
salt & pepper

TO SERVE

6 cups **mixed salad greens, such as Boston, Romaine, green leaf or red leaf (see Technique)** 1.5 L

For the chicken salad, toss the chicken with the green onion, mayonnaise and vinegar in a bowl. Crumble and gently stir in the blue cheese and season to taste. Chill until ready to serve.

For the egg and bacon salad, whisk the vinegar with the chives and mustard. Slowly whisk in the olive oil and season lightly. Grate the eggs on the coarse side of a box grater into a bowl. Gently stir in the vinaigrette and then the bacon. Chill until ready to serve.

For the tomato avocado salad, toss all the ingredients together in a bowl and season to taste. Chill until ready to serve.

To assemble, arrange the salad greens on individual plates. Spoon each of the three salads over the greens, keeping the salads separate.

Serves 6

TASTE Sometimes I like to make these salads independently. I'll spoon the chicken salad onto slices of walnut bread, spread the egg and bacon salad on toasted challah, and eat the tomato avocado salad with tortilla chips.

TECHNIQUE I prefer to make my own lettuce mix over buying the often limp, too-bitter premixed greens. I buy three types of lettuce, wash, tear and store it in resealable bags and find that it lasts for about a week. Considering we eat salad in our house just about every day, we definitely go through it that fast.

TALE My first introduction to Cobb salad was as a server at a Four Seasons Hotel. While it was the bestselling item on the menu, the salad isn't my strongest memory. The poolside café was called the "Cabana," and I'd always answer the phone with: "Hello, Cabana, Anna speaking." Cabana Anna was my nickname all summer.

DECONSTRUCTED WALDORF SALAD

When was the last time you made or ate a Waldorf salad? Apple, celery, walnuts and raisins all smothered in a creamy dressing—who can resist? To make Waldorf salad a little different, I layer the ingredients separately in a parfait glass or tumbler.

CREAMY DRESSING
¼ cup **mayonnaise** 60 mL
¼ cup **sour cream** 60 mL
1 tsp **minced garlic** 5 mL
salt & pepper

SALAD
4 cups **shredded iceberg lettuce** 1 L
1 **Granny Smith, McIntosh or Cortland apple, finely diced**
1 **celery stalk, sliced thinly on the bias**
1 **green onion, sliced thinly on the bias**
½ cup **golden raisins** 125 mL
½ cup **walnut pieces, lightly toasted** 125 mL

For the creamy dressing, stir together the mayonnaise, sour cream and garlic in a small bowl, then season to taste.

To arrange the salad, place a bit of iceberg lettuce at the bottom of 6 parfait glasses or large glass tumblers. Spoon a little creamy dressing over the lettuce. Sprinkle the diced apple into each glass, and then the celery, onion, raisins and walnuts. Top with a little dressing, then repeat the layers. Finish with a final sprinkling of raisins and walnut pieces on top as garnish.

Serves 6

TASTE I love the flavor and texture contrasts built into a regular Waldorf salad, but I do like deconstructing it as well so that I can appreciate each component on its own. I also find this version a little more colorful.

TECHNIQUE Most apples discolor within an hour of cutting, and tossing with a little lemon juice is the most common and most effective means to slow down the browning. If you can get your hands on Cortland apples, they are the ultimate salad apples—their snowy white interior hardly loses its glow, and they have an ideal texture for salads.

TALE I must have a thing for fruit salads. My mom saved my handwritten recipe for a fruit salad that I must have written when I was five or six years old. In the method, I write about "cinumin sprikled" on top of the fruit. Thank goodness for spell-check now!

CELERY ROOT, APPLE & ONION SLAW

This is almost like another twist on Waldorf salad, except this time I use vinaigrette instead of a creamy dressing, and also celery root, which has a milder taste than regular celery and a hint of creaminess in its texture.

For the vinaigrette, whisk the vinegar, honey, garlic, mustard and paprika in a small bowl. Gradually whisk in the oil until incorporated and season.

To peel the celery root, first cut off a section at the base to provide a flat surface. Using a chef's knife, cut off the peel from top to bottom a section at a time, wasting as little as possible. Then on a clean cutting board, cut the celery root into thin, matchstick pieces (or julienne on a kitchen mandolin—see Technique). In a medium-sized bowl, toss the celery root with a little lemon juice. Cut the apples into matchsticks of the same size, and thinly slice the onion, adding to the bowl with the celery root. Toss all the ingredients with the vinaigrette, adjust the seasoning and chill until ready to serve.

The salad can be prepared up to 6 hours before serving. *Serves 6*

VINAIGRETTE
2 Tbsp **apple cider vinegar** 30 mL
2 tsp **honey** 10 mL
1 tsp **minced garlic** 5 mL
½ tsp **dry mustard** 2 mL
¼ tsp **paprika** 1 mL
5 Tbsp **vegetable oil** 75 mL
salt & pepper

SLAW
1½ lb **celery root** 750 g
dash **lemon juice**
2 **Granny Smith or Cortland apples**
¼ **medium red onion**

TASTE Celery root truly does lend a creamy texture to dishes. I like to boil celery root with potatoes for mashing, and our neighbor when I was growing up, Ingrid Wilkins, used to make a fabulous celery root beet salad at holiday time, the celery root a lovely complement to the beets.

TECHNIQUE A mandolin is an indispensable chef's tool. After you've peeled away the coarse exterior of the celery root, the julienne blade attachment to this slicer makes perfect matchsticks. But note: if you're a first-time mandolin user, make use of the guard attachment—I've nicked my thumb too many times to count.

TALE The first time I decided to make a recipe with celery root, I was fresh out of university and not familiar with it other than in Ingrid's salad. I first made a mistake by buying kohlrabi (I knew as soon as that cabbage aroma hit me that I'd bought the wrong item), then next I bought salsify (I didn't know what to do with that either). Finally I swallowed my pride and asked the greengrocer to help me, and celery root is now a regular tenant in my fridge.

CUCUMBER THREE WAYS
Too often, cucumber ends up a component of plain old Tuesday night salad, right next to the diced tomato and red onion. But it deserves a place of its own on a salad plate, I feel. It's up to you if you wish to serve these salads independently or as a trio.

CUCUMBER WITH RASPBERRY & MINT
1 **English cucumber**
2 tsp **raspberry vinegar** 10 mL
1 tsp **sugar** 5 mL
salt & pepper
½ cup **fresh raspberries** 125 mL
1 Tbsp **chopped fresh mint** 15 mL

Thinly slice the cucumber. Toss with the vinegar and sugar and season. Let cucumber sit for an hour chilled.

Dish the cucumbers onto a serving plate with a slotted spoon (see Technique) and sprinkle with fresh raspberries and chopped mint.

CUCUMBER WITH SOUR CREAM, LIME & BASIL
1 **English cucumber**
2 Tbsp **sour cream** 30 mL
1 tsp **finely grated lime zest** 5 mL
2 tsp **lime juice** 10 mL
salt & pepper
2 Tbsp **chopped fresh basil** 30 mL

Thinly slice the cucumber and toss with sour cream and lime zest and juice. Season to taste. Immediately before serving, stir in the basil.

CUCUMBER WITH CHILI & GINGER
1 **English cucumber**
1 tsp **coarse salt** 5 mL
1 tsp **Sriracha sauce** 5 mL
1 tsp **finely grated ginger** 5 mL

Thinly slice the cucumber and toss with salt, Sriracha and ginger. Chill the cucumber for 1 to 2 hours, then squeeze out excess water (see Technique) before serving. *Each salad serves 6*

TASTE I think of cucumber as one of those neutral but elegant vegetables. Like romaine lettuce, it is refreshingly crunchy, and is a great foil for other flavors. I had to include at least three styles of cucumber salad.

TECHNIQUE Once a cucumber is sliced, it keeps letting out water. If you wish to prepare your cucumber salads a day ahead, it's best to first sprinkle the sliced cucumber with a little coarse salt and a splash of rice vinegar. Place the cucumbers in a strainer over a bowl in the fridge for a few hours before mixing it with the dressing. Then the flavor of your salad won't be diluted by cucumber water.

TALE I've never been much of a gardener (but I very much appreciate the art of it and the skill in others). I do, however, recall as a child my fascination with the cucumber vine that grew on our fence. With its gripping tendrils, and yellow blossoms, the vine ultimately yielded green crunchy cukes. We should remind ourselves how important it is to be enthralled and interested in where our food comes from.

TURKEY SALAD WITH DRIED APRICOT & MARJORAM

I find that chicken or turkey salad always needs that little "something" to make it more interesting. Dried apricots, a hint of lemon and a sprinkling of poppy seeds—now that's interesting *and* tasty.

TO POACH THE TURKEY
1 **medium onion, peeled and cut in half**
1 **lemon, cut in half**
2 **bay leaves**
2 **sprigs marjoram**
1 **turkey breast, about 1½ lb (750 g)**

THE SALAD
½ cup **chopped dried apricots** 125 mL
1 Tbsp **lemon juice** 15 mL
½ cup **mayonnaise** 125 mL
½ cup **yogurt** 125 mL
¼ cup **finely diced red onion** 60 mL
2 tsp **chopped fresh marjoram** 10 mL
2 tsp **poppy seeds** 10 mL
salt & pepper
Boston lettuce leaves, for serving

To cook the turkey, bring 6 cups (1.5 L) of water to a simmer over medium heat with the onion, lemon, bay leaves and marjoram. Add the turkey breast and cook, uncovered, keeping the poaching liquid just below a simmer (see Technique). Cook until the turkey reaches an internal temperature of 175°F (80°C), about 20 minutes. Remove the turkey from the poaching liquid, cool to room temperature and dice into ½-inch (1 cm) cubes.

For the turkey salad, steep the dried apricots in lemon juice and 2 Tbsp (30 mL) hot water until absorbed. In a medium bowl stir the mayonnaise, yogurt, onion, marjoram and poppy seeds. Stir in the diced turkey and apricots, and season to taste. Chill until ready to serve.

Serve spooned onto Boston leaves. *Serves 4*

TASTE You could certainly serve this turkey salad in a traditional fashion on bread (multigrain would be best, I think), but spooning it onto Boston lettuce leaves is pretty and less filling. You can also pick up the lettuce leaves and eat this by hand.

TECHNIQUE Poaching is an easy, healthy and flavorful cooking technique. It's amazing how just that bit of onion, lemon and bay infuses the turkey as it cooks. A true poach should be just below a simmer so as to not over-cook the outside of the meat before the center is done. In the case of fish, poaching is a gentle method to keep the fish from falling apart, which it would if the liquid were at a higher heat.

TALE In the '60s and '70s, a hip chicken salad had celery and paprika. In the '80s, it was all about grapes and curry powder. In the '90s, it was olives and sun-dried tomatoes. And now, for the 21st century, it's apricots and poppy seeds that make a chicken salad *cool*!

FIVE-BEAN SALAD

Why have three-bean or even four-bean, when you can have, count 'em, *five*-bean salad? And this is nothing like the drab bean salad you buy at the deli counter—this salad is fresh, vibrant and even crunchy!

½ lb **fresh green beans, stems trimmed** 250 g

½ lb **fresh yellow wax beans** 250 g

1 can **(14 oz/398 mL) black beans, drained and rinsed**

1 can **(14 oz/398 mL) white kidney beans, drained and rinsed**

1 can **(14 oz/398 mL) romano beans, drained and rinsed OR** 1 lb **fresh romano beans, in their shell** 500 g

½ **sweet onion (such as Vidalia), thinly sliced**

½ cup **thinly sliced celery (or 2 tsp/10 mL chopped fresh lovage)** 125 mL

¼ cup **raspberry vinegar** 60 mL

1 Tbsp **finely chopped fresh thyme** 15 mL

2 Tbsp **olive oil** 30 mL

salt & pepper

For the green and yellow beans, have a bowl of ice water ready. Blanch the green beans in boiling salted water until just tender, about 5 minutes, then drain and shock in ice water (see Technique). Repeat with the yellow beans—they take about a minute less. Drain. Cut the beans on the bias into 1-inch (2.5 cm) pieces.

In a large bowl, toss the green and yellow beans with the black beans, white kidney beans and romano beans. If you are using fresh romano beans, shell them and simmer in salted water for 20 minutes, then drain and cool. Add the onion and celery (or chopped lovage). Add the vinegar, thyme and olive oil and toss to coat. Season to taste and chill until ready to serve.

Salad can be dressed and chilled for up to 6 hours before serving.

Serves 8

TASTE There are two herbs in particular that are favorites of mine and that pop up every year in my garden: lovage, which has an intense celery taste (in fact I use the seeds from the flowering stems in my chili sauce [page 199]), and lemon thyme, which I use interchangeably with regular thyme in recipes.

TECHNIQUE I like to cook green and yellow beans just until they soften a little. In this salad I also like them to have a little crunch. After they've hit the perfect degree of doneness (and I test by tasting), I shock them in ice water to immediately halt the cooking, and also to set the bright color.

TALE I like fresh romano beans from the market—the shells have that same mottled red and white color like the beans inside them. It's too bad that, once cooked, they lose their tiger stripes and turn into a ruddy red color.

[SANDWICHES]

Do sandwiches deserve a chapter all on their own? They sure do. I do love a good sandwich, but I can fall into a sandwich rut as easily as everyone else.

Too often a sandwich is merely regarded as a source of fuel, something we throw together when we can't think of anything else to make. But it doesn't have to lack originality—a sandwich can be a form of self-expression and maybe even a work of art! Its portability and convenience are also great reasons to create a sandwich, making it perfect for a packed lunch and for picnics.

PROSCIUTTO & GORGONZOLA ON BAGUETTE WITH PEAR & FIG

It seems every Western culture has a ham sandwich—it's one of those things that's just around, but it needn't be taken for granted. North Americans enjoy a classic Black Forest ham with cheddar, the French have "jambon" on crusty baguette, the Spanish have *bocadillo de jamón*—ham on a crusty roll. Any way you slice it, it's a classic. Here's one that has more of an Italian inspiration behind it.

Divide the baguette into 4, then slice each piece in half lengthwise. Spread Dijon on the inside of each and ruffle slices of prosciutto onto the baguette (3 slices per sandwich). Slice the pear thinly and lay over the prosciutto, and do the same with the figs. Crumble gorgonzola over the fig slices and top with the other half of the baguette, pressing gently.

These sandwiches can be served as is, perhaps wrapped and packed for lunches or picnics, or they can be served warm, pressed on a panini press (see Technique). *Serves 4*

1 **fresh crusty baguette**
4 tsp **Dijon mustard** 20 mL
12 slices **prosciutto ham**
1 **ripe Bartlett pear**
2 **fresh figs**
3 oz **Gorgonzola cheese** 90 g

TASTE Gorgonzola is a creamy blue cheese with a fruity, strong finish to it. The saltiness of the prosciutto and the sweetness of the fruits temper it a bit, but if blue cheese is not your thing, brie is a perfect replacement.

TECHNIQUE This sandwich also heats very nicely. Use a panini press if you have one, or simply wrap the sandwich in foil and bake in a 350°F (180°C) oven for about 10 minutes.

TALE I went to cooking school in Vail, Colorado, so in addition to learning about fine cuisine I got to ski a whole lot, too. My favorite lunch I took traveling up the chairlift to the top of the mountain was this sandwich, which I ordered at a small French café at the base of the lift. Talk about living the life!

HAM & HERBED CREAM CHEESE ON RAISIN BREAD

This is the new, modern ham and cheese sandwich. Using raisin bread may seem strange at first, but it will win you over. This sandwich makes a great companion to a bowl of Canadian Minestrone (page 12).

HERBED CREAM CHEESE

8 oz **cream cheese, at room temperature** 250 g

2 Tbsp **finely chopped green onion or chives** 30 mL

1 Tbsp **chopped fresh oregano** 15 mL

¼ tsp **ground black pepper** 1 mL

FOR THE SANDWICH

8 slices **raisin bread (preferably without too much cinnamon)**

12 oz **good quality ham, thinly sliced** 375 g

For the herbed cream cheese, beat the cream cheese in a small bowl to soften. Add the green onion or chives, oregano and pepper and stir until blended.

To assemble the sandwiches, spread the herbed cream cheese on all of the raisin bread slices. Arrange the ham on the cream cheese, sandwich the bread together and slice in half.

Another tasty option: toasting the raisin bread before assembling.

Serves 4

TASTE Buy raisin bread that doesn't have too much cinnamon in it, although a little is all right. Buying good quality Black Forest ham is equally important—nothing too salty or watery.

TECHNIQUE The herbed cream cheese can be made easily in a food processor, and the cream cheese will take on a nice, herbaceous green color. I also like to use this cream cheese for a sandwich with Genoa salami.

TALE My inspiration for this sandwich is Easter Breakfast. When I was growing up, our family made a bigger production out of Easter breakfast than dinner—we still do today. We had a whole roasted ham (which cooked slowly overnight), beets with horseradish, hard-boiled eggs, and many egg-y Easter breads, including *Paska* with raisins, which is a Slovak tradition. I would always make a sandwich with ham slices and the Paska, not just at breakfast but for days after.

CHICKEN CORDON BLEU PANINI

I don't make chicken Cordon Bleu too often at home, though my husband and I both love it. This sandwich version seems much easier and quells the cravings.

For the garlic dressing, blend the mayonnaise, sour cream and garlic and season to taste.

For the paninis, lay out the bread slices and spread the garlic dressing on each slice. Arrange the sliced chicken and ham on 4 slices, and top with spinach leaves and Swiss cheese. Cover with remaining bread slices.

Preheat a panini press and cook the paninis about 8 minutes, or until the cheese is melted. (Or heat a large sauté pan with 1 Tbsp [15 mL] olive oil over medium heat. Weigh down the paninis with a heavy lid and turn the paninis over halfway through.)

Slice the paninis in half and serve immediately. *Serves 4*

GARLIC DRESSING
¼ cup **mayonnaise** 60 mL
¼ cup **sour cream** 60 mL
1 clove **garlic, minced**
salt & pepper

FOR THE PANINIS
8 slices **multigrain bread**
1 lb **cooked chicken meat, sliced or shredded** 500 g
4 slices **Black Forest ham**
2 cups **spinach leaves, washed and trimmed** 500 mL
4 slices **Swiss Emmenthal cheese**

TASTE This panini version of Cordon Bleu accomplishes everything of its original counterpart. The multigrain bread gets crispy and toasted on the outside, just like the breadcrumb coating, the garlic dressing replaces the garlic or herb butter of the original, and the Swiss cheese? Well, melted Swiss in or on just about anything is a winner.

TECHNIQUE Mayonnaise turns oily and greasy when heated, but blending it with sour cream lowers the fat content and keeps the dressing creamy. You can use low-fat mayo and low-fat sour cream in this recipe if you wish.

TALE This is one of our all-time bestselling sandwiches at our bakeries. It's also a favorite with the staff, too.

CHILI SHRIMP TOSTADAS

These tostadas are a Mexican version of an open-faced sandwich. Making tortillas from scratch keeps the sandwiches dainty and easy to pick up and eat.

TORTILLAS

1½ cups **masa harina (a Mexican corn flour—see Taste)** 375 mL **OR**
1 cup (250 mL) **cornmeal plus** ½ cup (125 mL) **all-purpose flour**
½ tsp **fine salt** 2 mL
1¼ cups **warm water** 310 mL
oil, for greasing pan

SHRIMP

1½ lb **cooked and peeled shrimp (31/40 or cooked salad shrimp)** 750 g
1 cup **cooked black beans, drained and rinsed** 250 mL
⅔ cup **chili sauce (see page 199), or prepared salsa** 160 mL
¼ cup **chopped fresh cilantro** 60 mL
dash **hot sauce (optional)**
3 oz **feta cheese** 90 g
2 cups **shredded iceberg lettuce** 500 mL
½ cup **sour cream** 125 mL

For the tortillas, in a bowl mix the masa harina (or cornmeal and flour), salt and water to make a thick paste—it will become thicker and more doughlike as it continues to sit.

Heat a nonstick pan over medium heat and add a scant teaspoon (5 mL) of oil. Shape about 2 Tbsp (30 mL) of the masa mixture into a ball and place inside a resealable bag. Press the bag flat with a heavy pot until the tortilla is very thin, about 5 inches (12 cm) in diameter (see Technique). (Or use a tortilla press, if you have one!) Place the tortilla in a hot fry pan and cook for 2 minutes on each side. Remove from the heat to cool. Repeat with the remaining masa mix, adding a teaspoon (5 mL) of oil each you cook a tortilla.

For the shrimp, preheat the oven to 400°F (200°C). Chop the shrimp into bite-sized pieces and toss with the black beans, chili sauce (or prepared salsa), cilantro and hot sauce, if using. Place the tortillas on a parchment-lined baking sheet and spoon the shrimp mixture on each. Crumble feta over the shrimp and bake for 10 minutes. Lift the tostadas onto a serving plate and top with shredded lettuce and sour cream.

Makes 12 tostadas • Serves 6

TASTE Masa harina is a corn flour, but has a particular fragrance and taste to it that is distinctively Mexican. It is available in most grocery stores, in the flour section or the ethnic section. I also use masa harina to coat fish for pan-frying, or in place of cornmeal in cornbread.

TECHNIQUE Make the tortilla as flat and thin as possible. You can roll them on a floured work surface with a rolling pin if you wish, but try not to add too much of the masa flour when rolling. Shape the tortilla and cook immediately one at a time; if you shape them all first, the dough dries out and they crack when rolled or pressed any further.

TALE My first introduction to masa harina was when I ate my first authentic Mexican tamale, a corn husk–wrapped specialty filled with soft masa (cooked like polenta) and a rich, spicy meat mixture. A group of us drove for miles out into the Hill Country of Texas outside Austin, and out in the middle of the desert was this small but packed Mexican restaurant. We left so full and happy—definitely worth the drive.

BEEF, CARAMELIZED ONION & SMOKED CHEDDAR ON FOCACCIA

This is a great sandwich to make from leftovers after a Sunday supper. You can even assemble it as you are packing away the leftovers, so that lunch is packed for Monday. (See, there is a reason to look forward to Mondays.)

For the caramelized onions, heat the oil and butter over medium heat in a heavy-bottomed sauté pan. Add the onions and cook, uncovered, stirring occasionally until the onions are a rich golden brown—this should take about 40 minutes (reduce the heat if they are browning too quickly—see Technique below and on page 5). Stir in the sherry and season.

Preheat the panini press (or preheat the oven to 375°F [190°C]).

To build the sandwiches, slice each portion of focaccia in half. Spread grainy mustard on both sides. Ruffle the roast beef slices on one side and spoon a generous heaping spoonful of the caramelized onions on the beef. Top with the smoked cheddar and then the focaccia half.

Put the sandwiches in the panini press until the cheese is melted. (Or wrap each sandwich in foil and heat in the oven for about 15 minutes, or until the cheese is melted and the outside of focaccia is toasty.) Slice each sandwich in half and serve. *Serves 4*

CARAMELIZED ONIONS
1 Tbsp **olive oil** 15 mL
1 Tbsp **butter** 15 mL
4 **medium onions, sliced**
2 Tbsp **dry sherry** 30 mL
salt & pepper

FOR THE SANDWICH
1 loaf **focaccia (with herbed topping), cut into 4 portions**
4 Tbsp **coarse grainy mustard** 60 mL
12 oz **thinly sliced roast beef, preferably leftovers from Pot Roast (see page 107)** 375 g
3 oz **sliced (or grated) smoked cheddar** 90 g

TASTE What wins me over with this really simple sandwich is the flavor mingling of two of my favorite, classic dishes: French onion soup (see page 5 for my recipe) and pot roast (page 107).

TECHNIQUE Don't rush the onions. Caramelized onions cooked over too high a heat will brown, yes, but they will lack the depth of flavor that comes from slowly caramelizing the sugars *within* the onion.

TALE This sandwich appears seasonally on my bakery menus and attracts a regular following. A few customers come in and order it at the end of the day for dinner—now that's satisfying takeout.

SAMOSA SANDWICHES
Samosas make for a great spicy snack, but this vegetarian sandwich becomes a whole meal, and plays up those fragrant Indian flavors.

FILLING
2½ cups **peeled and diced Yukon Gold potatoes (½-inch/1 cm dice)** 625 mL

1 Tbsp **whole fennel seeds** 15 mL

1 Tbsp **whole cumin seeds** 15 mL

2 tsp **whole coriander seeds, coarsely cracked** 10 mL

3 Tbsp **vegetable oil** 45 mL

½ cup **finely diced onion** 125 mL

2 cloves **garlic, minced**

1-inch piece **fresh ginger, peeled and grated** 2.5 cm piece

1 can **(14 oz/398 mL) chickpeas, drained and rinsed**

1 pkg **(1 lb/500 g) frozen spinach, thawed and excess juices squeezed out**

½ cup **frozen peas, thawed** 125 mL

salt & pepper

FOR THE SANDWICHES
6 **pita pockets, white or whole wheat**

Mango Chutney (see page 205)

For the filling, boil the diced potatoes uncovered in salted water until tender, about 15 minutes, then drain well and set aside.

In a large sauté pan over medium heat, toast the fennel, cumin and coriander seeds for 2 minutes, or until fragrant. Add the oil and then the onion and sauté for 4 minutes, or until translucent. Add the garlic and ginger and sauté 1 minute more. Stir in the chickpeas, spinach, peas and cooked potatoes. Get tough with it—mash up the potatoes while stirring so that all the ingredients stick together. (It's easier to spoon the mixture into the pita.) Season to taste.

Split open the pita pockets and spoon in the warm filling (see Technique). Serve with Mango Chutney on the side. *Serves 6*

TASTE Honestly, I'm not a big fan of fennel seed in Italian dishes, but I love its nutty, licorice flavor in Indian dishes. I sometimes make the samosa filling as a side dish to grilled chicken or fish, serving the mango chutney alongside as well.

TECHNIQUE To make it easier to eat, I like to fold the pita like a falafel sandwich— I split the pita open halfway along the seam, spoon the filling in the bottom half and tuck in one "flap" of the pita over the filling, pressing gently to secure. Then I tightly roll up the entire sandwich. You can always spoon a little of the mango chutney into the pita before wrapping, if you wish.

TALE I first learned to make samosas from the owner of the deli and cheese shop where I worked as a teenager. She also taught me to make hummus, baba ganouj, tabbouleh salad and falafel. I wonder what my after-school staff will remember about their first job working for me?

ALMOND BUTTER, HONEY & BANANA ON CHALLAH BREAD (A.K.A. THE VEGAS ELVIS)

A childhood favorite elevated to adult standards, this sandwich takes Elvis's peanut butter and banana sandwich and glitzes it up Vegas-style. Thank ya, thank ya very much!

Spread slices of challah or egg bread with almond butter. Drizzle honey over the almond butter. Slice bananas on an angle and arrange over the almond butter and honey. Sprinkle lightly with cinnamon and top with the other half of bread. Slice in half and enjoy with a cold glass of milk!

For a superdecadent treat dip the sandwiches in an egg-milk mixture and fry as you would French toast. You could even sprinkle a few chocolate chips in the sandwich. *Serves 4*

8 slices **challah or other fresh egg bread**
½ cup **pure toasted almond butter** 125 mL
¼ cup **clover honey** 60 mL
2 **ripe but firm bananas**
pinch **ground cinnamon**

TASTE Almond butter is my new peanut butter. Almonds are just about the most virtuous nut, containing Vitamin E, magnesium and calcium—research even shows that almonds can lower bad cholesterol (LDL). I like that almond butter is available in pure form (no added sugar or emulsifiers). It's just the best on toast in the morning.

TECHNIQUE The "technique" here is really all about simplicity. If your kids eat nut butters, then this is a great one to have them make.

TALE The original peanut butter version of this sandwich was one of my favorites in a packed lunch—the bread never went soggy, it didn't matter if the sandwich got squished between the apple and the juice box and it didn't have to stay cold.

THE HENLEY VEGGIE SANDWICH This
sandwich is named after the Royal Canadian Henley Regatta, the local version of the British regatta held in Niagara. The sandwich made its debut on the menu at the bakery during this spectacular athletic weekend.

Lightly toast the walnut pieces in a sauté pan over medium heat and toss until browned slightly, about 5 minutes. Cool.

Pulse the walnut pieces in a food processor with the basil, parsley and salt. Add the garlic, ginger and orange zest and pulse again. Add the olive oil in a thin stream with the machine running. Set aside. (If preparing this beforehand, chill in the refrigerator, but take it out an hour before serving.)

For the veggies, cut the eggplant and zucchini lengthwise into ¼-inch-thick (6 mm) slices. Cut the red pepper into quarters removing the seeds, and slice the onion into ½-inch (1 cm) rounds. On a grill pan (or on a barbecue), grill the veggies without oil on medium-high heat, about 4 minutes on each side. Place the veggies in a bowl and cover with plastic wrap—this will finish cooking the veggies without them getting soggy. After 10 minutes, unwrap the bowl, stir in 3 Tbsp (45 mL) of pesto and season to taste.

To build the sandwiches, preheat the panini press (or preheat the oven to 375°F [190°C]). Split open the panini buns or pitas, spread a little pesto on the bread and fill with veggies. Slice the bocconcini and place inside. Put the sandwiches in the panini press (or wrap in foil and bake in the oven) until the cheese has melted. Serve warm. *Serves 4*

WALNUT PESTO
1 cup **walnut pieces** 250 mL
1 cup **fresh basil, loosely packed** 250 mL
½ cup **fresh parsley, loosely packed** 125 mL
¾ tsp **fine salt** 4 mL
1 clove **garlic, minced**
1 tsp **finely minced ginger** 5 mL
1 tsp **finely grated orange zest** 5 mL
⅓ cup **olive oil** 80 mL

GRILLED VEGGIES
1 **small eggplant**
1 **green zucchini**
1 **red bell pepper**
1 **small red onion**
salt & pepper

FOR THE SANDWICHES
4 **panini buns or whole wheat pitas**
4 oz **bocconcini cheese** 125 g

TASTE Walnut pesto is an easy way to add protein to a vegetarian sandwich. The pesto freezes well, too. And goat cheese is an appealing substitute for the bocconcini, if you prefer.

TECHNIQUE A traditional pesto has basil, garlic, Parmesan and pine nuts. But now there are so many variations that it seems any herb puréed with other ingredients can be called a "pesto." In this recipe, the ginger and garlic give it an almost Asian kick. Be sure to mince it before putting it in the food processor. I have found if I put it in whole it never processes finely enough (and I'm always the one who bites into the big piece!).

TALE You have never seen so many fit, young, beautiful people as you do on Henley weekend. You can't be a rower, though, and be embarrassed about your weight. They weigh you the morning of your race and stamp your weight on your arm like a tattoo for all to see. This may explain why the rowers come for the veggie sandwich at the bakery the day before the race, and come back for the cookies the day after!

[APPETIZERS & LIGHT ENTRÉES]

When I go out to eat, especially to a restaurant I love or have been meaning to try for ages, I find two things usually happen. Firstly, I have trouble deciding *what* to eat (the sign of a good menu?). Secondly, my small appetite makes me steer clear of full portion entrées—even if the sauces and sides sound so appealing, I know I have trouble eating a full portion of lamb rack, a venison chop or a 12-ounce steak. To satisfy myself, I tend to order multiple appetizers so I can get a taste of everything and not feel stuffed at the end of the meal.

That is why I have created a chapter "appetizers *and* light entrées"—they can be one and the same. Some of the hors d'oeuvres can also be a small meal in themselves, and vice versa—some of the light entrées can be cut into bite-sized pieces and become perfect hors d'oeuvres.

I do find that most small servings are also appealing to the eye. As an hors d'oeuvre or appetizer, these dishes are the first peek of your menu—sort of the red-carpet entrance to your dinner party. Take the time to choose the serving plates, and don't forget to garnish.

ULTIMATE CHEESE FONDUE

I'm not taking liberties with this classic—just giving you a great recipe that stands the test of time. A good cheese fondue is not difficult to make, but the quality of the cheese does count.

1 clove **garlic**
1 bottle **dry white wine (3 cups/750 mL)**
3 cups **grated Swiss Gruyère** 750 mL
3 cups **grated Swiss Emmenthal** 750 mL

2 cups **grated medium Gouda** 500 mL
2 Tbsp **cornstarch** 30 mL
1 oz **kirsch (cherry brandy)** 30 mL
day-old baguette, cut into cubes for dipping

Smash the garlic clove and rub it on the bottom and sides of a fondue pot and a medium, heavy-bottomed pot. Pour the wine in the pot and bring to just below a simmer over medium heat. In a bowl, toss the cheeses with the cornstarch. Reduce the heat to medium-low and add the cheese in 2 additions, stirring gently with a wooden spoon until melted and it just begins to bubble and becomes smoother. Stir in the kirsch, and transfer the fondue to the fondue pot. Serve with baguette pieces. *Serves 6*

TASTE All right, I have made a slight change to the classic cheese fondue—everything except the Gouda is true to the original. I like the Gruyère and Emmenthal for stretchiness and that earthy Swiss flavor, but a good medium Gouda—a nice Dutch cheese—adds a zip and a creaminess that can't be beat.

TECHNIQUE Warm the fondue pot before pouring in the cheese mixture by placing it over the heat so that the fondue keeps its smooth and velvety viscosity from the stovetop.

TALE I have a bottle of kirsch that sits at the back of my cupboard and comes out for special moments like fondue night. Other uses for kirsch? Brush it on a homemade Black Forest cake, drizzle it over ripe, sweet bing cherries, sprinkle it over scalloped potatoes with cheese (and it will give it a fondue taste!) . . . Good thing kirsch comes in a small bottle.

MUSHROOMS IN GREEN PEPPERCORN CREAM ON CROSTINI

Any mix of mushrooms will do, but of the "wild" mushrooms, cremini, oyster and shiitake may be the most readily available. Even button mushrooms can be superstars when enveloped in cream spiked with briny green peppercorns.

Melt the butter in a large sauté pan over medium-high heat. Add the mushrooms and sauté until tender and almost all the liquid has evaporated, about 5 minutes (see Technique). Add the shallot, thyme and green peppercorns and cook 1 minute. Stir in the brandy and then the cream. Reduce the cream for a minute or 2, until thickened slightly. Season to taste.

While the mushrooms are cooking, prepare the crostini. Preheat the oven to 400°F (200°C). Slice 6 very long, thin slices of baguette on the bias. Spread a little butter on each slice and toast on a baking sheet until just golden and crispy.

To serve, place a crostini on each plate and spoon the mushrooms over each one. *Serves 6*

1 Tbsp **butter, plus extra for crostini** 15 mL

2 lb **mixed mushrooms, including cremini, oyster and shiitake, sliced** 1 kg

1 **shallot, minced**

1 tsp **chopped fresh thyme** 5 mL

2 Tbsp **green peppercorns in brine, drained** 30 mL

2 Tbsp **brandy** 30 mL

1 cup **whipping cream (35%)** 250 mL

salt & pepper
day-old baguette

TASTE Earthy and subdued, this starter would make an unctuous precursor to a grilled steak. In fact, you could skip the crostini and serve the mushrooms on top of the steak!

TECHNIQUE A great mushroom dish lies in the cooking of the mushrooms. High heat is key to lightly caramelize the exterior of the sliced mushrooms and quickly evaporate the excess water. The mineral essence of the mushrooms shines through this way. If portobello mushrooms tickle your fancy, using them is fine, but remember to scrape off the black gills before cooking or they will discolor your cream sauce.

TALE If you have access to deluxe mushrooms such as morels, chanterelles, black trumpets or hedgehogs, please use them in this recipe—you are lucky, indeed. But remember, don't go mushroom hunting in the forest without an expert. Michael and I once met a mycologist (a mushroom scientist) who boasted a sign on his door, "There are old mycologists and there are bold mycologists, but there are no old, bold mycologists." Point taken.

CRÊPES FLORENTINE

Anything "Florentine" means it typically has spinach as a key ingredient. Am I missing something, though? Does it mean that Florence is the spinach capital of the world? No matter—I think our taste for spinach dip has roots in this creamy crêpe dish.

CRÊPES

3 **large eggs**

1½ cups **2% milk** 375 mL

1⅔ cups **all-purpose flour** 410 mL

1 Tbsp **sugar** 15 mL

¼ tsp **fine salt** 1 mL

2 Tbsp **vegetable oil** 30 mL

1 cup **light ale lager beer or club soda** 250 mL

vegetable oil, for greasing the pan

FILLING AND SAUCE

1 Tbsp **butter** 15 mL

3 Tbsp **finely chopped shallots** 45 mL

1 lb **fresh spinach, stems trimmed** 500 g

¼ tsp **ground nutmeg** 1 mL

salt & pepper

8 oz **cream cheese, at room temperature** 250 g

1 tsp **finely grated lemon zest** 5 mL

1 tsp **Dijon mustard** 5 mL

8 oz **cooked salad shrimp or crabmeat** 250 g

1 cup **whipping cream (35%)** 250 mL

⅓ cup **dry breadcrumbs** 80 mL

⅓ cup **finely grated Parmesan cheese** 80 mL

For the crêpes, whisk the eggs and milk in a bowl to combine and then whisk in the flour, sugar and salt (or pulse in a food processor or blender). Let sit for 15 minutes (or cover and chill until ready to use), then stir in the oil and beer or club soda.

Put a sheet of parchment on a baking sheet for the cooked crêpes. Heat a crêpe pan or other large nonstick pan over medium heat and grease lightly. Ladle 2 to 3 Tbsp (30 to 45 mL) of the batter into the center of the pan and swirl to coat a thin, even layer. Cook just until the surface of the crêpe looks dry and the edges curl up a little. Flip the crêpe over and cook 30 seconds before removing to the baking sheet to cool. (You can let them overlap, but stacking them will make them too soggy.) Repeat with the remaining batter, adjusting the heat if necessary. After they cool, wrap them in plastic wrap, and store at room temperature if using the same day, or freeze for later use (do not refrigerate).

For the filling, heat a large sauté pan over high heat and melt the butter. Add the shallots and cook 3 minutes. Add the spinach and cook, turning often, until wilted. Stir in the nutmeg and season lightly. Let cool to room temperature.

In a food processor blend the cream cheese until smooth and then add the cooled spinach, lemon zest and mustard. Divide the mixture into 2 bowls, and stir in the shrimp or crabmeat into one, adjusting seasoning if needed. Reserve the other half for the sauce.

To assemble, preheat the oven to 375°F (190°C). Lay out 4 crêpes onto a work surface. Pipe or spoon about ¼ cup (60 mL) of the seafood spinach mixture in a line on each crêpe. Roll up the crêpe and place in a lightly greased 9- x 13-inch (3.5 L) baking dish. Repeat with the remaining crêpes.

For the sauce, whisk in the whipping cream into the remaining spinach and cream cheese mixture and pour over the crêpes. Combine the bread-crumbs and Parmesan and sprinkle on top. Bake uncovered for 30 minutes, or until browned and bubbling around the edges. Let sit for 5 minutes before serving. *Makes 12 crêpes • Serves 6 as an appetizer, 4 as an entrée*

TASTE The beer or club soda is a key ingredient in good crêpes, not because it imparts flavor but because the bubbles create tiny air pockets in the crêpe as it cooks, making them tender and light.

TECHNIQUE Making a good crêpe takes getting the heat just right and, if you're using a cast iron and/or crêpe pan, a well-seasoned one. The first crêpe is always awful, no matter how good you are at making them. And flipping them without a utensil? Without a step-by-step diagram, the best bit of advice I have to offer is that the flip is not in the wrist, but in the elbow. To flip a crêpe (or to sauté like the chefs do), it takes a quick motion forward and back, not up and down. The crêpe will slide up the far side of the pan and flip itself over. Not sure about that? Practice first with a slice of bread. Crêpe making is a great lesson in physics!

TALE Oh how I loved going to the Magic Pan restaurant when I was a kid. I would watch with fascination as the rotating crêpe machine would slowly spin over an element, while the special "Crêpe Chef" (probably a morose 17-year-old working after school) would dip the bottoms of the pan in the crêpe batter and pull them off as they completed their tour around the wheel. My order every time: salad with tinned clementine oranges and toasted almonds, Crêpes Florentine, and Crêpes Cherries Royale for dessert. How elegant, I thought!

ARTICHOKE ASIAGO SQUARES

Love that artichoke dip? You know, the stuff you can serve warm or chilled? Well, these hors d'oeuvre squares taste just like the dip, and are much easier to pick up and eat. If there is no other recipe you make from this book, please make this one.

2 cups **marinated artichokes (from a jar), drained** 500 mL

1 cup **frozen chopped spinach, thawed and squeezed** 250 mL

½ cup **diced onion** 125 mL

1 clove **garlic, minced**

1 Tbsp **chopped fresh oregano** 15 mL

2 Tbsp **lemon juice** 30 mL

4 **large eggs**

¼ cup **dry breadcrumbs** 60 mL

½ lb **grated Asiago cheese** 250 g

Preheat the oven to 350°F (180°C). Grease and line an 8-inch (2 L) square pan with parchment paper so that the paper hangs over the sides.

In a food processor, pulse the artichokes, spinach, onion, garlic and oregano until finely chopped but not puréed. Pulse in the lemon juice and eggs, and then the breadcrumbs and Asiago. Scrape the mixture into the prepared pan, spread to level and bake for 20 to 25 minutes or until set. Cool to room temperature before slicing into squares.

If you are preparing these beforehand, they can be served cold directly from the fridge, or they can be warmed for 8 minutes in a 325°F (160°C) oven. *Makes one 8-inch (2 L) square pan (25 squares)*

TASTE This treat is great served on its own, or as a base for shrimp, a slice of roast beef or chicken or even a little chili sauce (page 199).

TECHNIQUE There's not much to the technique here, only that the entire recipe can be made in a food processor so takes less than 15 minutes to make. That's just the ticket when making hors d'oeuvres. So many hors d'oeuvre recipes are quite fussy (and that's okay), but it's smart to throw a simple one into the mix.

TALE I adapted this recipe from a version my mom always makes. Every time we get together for a family occasion and Mom asks me what to bring, this is always what I request.

ASPARAGUS & CHIVE OMELETTE When
I'm working from home (where I do most of my writing), I'm most inclined to make an omelette for lunch. It takes no time at all to make, and I really enjoy a hot lunch.

Blanch asparagus in salted, boiling water until just tender, then drain and shock in ice water to halt cooking. Remove from the ice water and set aside.

Preheat the oven to 375°F (190°C).

Whisk the eggs and cream in a bowl until evenly blended. Heat a medium-sized ovenproof nonstick skillet (or omelette pan) over medium-high heat. Melt the butter in the skillet, then ladle in one-quarter of the egg mixture. Immediately begin stirring the eggs vigorously with a silicone spatula in circular motions, taking care to pull the eggs away from the outside edge of the pan. If the omelette is cooking too quickly, lift the pan off the heat while stirring, then return it to the heat. Once the egg starts setting enough that a solid edge is visible around the omelette, stop stirring. Place a few spears over the omelette, season lightly and place pan, uncovered, in the oven for 3 minutes.

Have a plate ready. Remove the pan from the oven (use a towel —the handle will be hot) and loosen the edges of the omelette with a spatula. Tilt the pan toward the plate and slide the spatula underneath the omelette from where it's closest to the handle. With a flip of your wrist, lift the omelette from the side so it starts turning over on itself. Let gravity do the rest, and let the omelette fall onto the plate so that it starts gently rolling over itself. Sprinkle the top of the omelette lightly with salt and pepper and generously with chives. Serve immediately while repeating with remaining eggs. *Serves 4*

[continued next page . . .]

1 lb **fresh asparagus** 500 g
8 **large eggs**
½ cup **whipping cream (35%)** 125 mL
butter, for the pan
salt & pepper
3 Tbsp **chopped fresh chives** 45 mL

TASTE In my mind, a good omelette is in the technique, and a properly made omelette doesn't need loads of fillings. The simplicity of the asparagus with chives is a natural choice for spring.

TECHNIQUE Practice, practice, practice. A well-made omelette should not be browned at all on the outside, so a good nonstick pan, preferably one with a rounded edge at the bottom, works best. (A crêpe pan can also work.) The step of putting it in the oven for just three minutes cooks it through just enough so you can gracefully fold it over itself and onto the plate without breaking. The practice is mostly about aiming the pan over the plate in the right place so that it falls where you want it to, and centering the omelette on the plate and hopefully not on the counter (or floor . . . or poochy gets a real treat).

TALE I learned my omelette skills at cooking school and from Michael, who got his omelette wisdom from cooking school as well as working at a French bistro as an apprentice. There are as many ways to make an omelette as there are people who make them. Everyone's an expert it seems, so long as you've had lots of practice.

MUSHROOM POTATO BRIE TARTS These
tarts make a lovely side dish for an entrée, or can be a light lunch accompanied by a salad.

Boil potatoes in salted water until just cooked, about 15 minutes, and drain well.

Heat 2 Tbsp (30 mL) olive oil in a medium sauté pan over medium-high heat and add mushrooms, garlic and shallot. Sauté until the mushrooms are tender, about 5 minutes, then add the vermouth, cooking until liquid has evaporated. Add in the cooked potato, heat through and season while warm (see Taste). Cool to room temperature, and then stir in the beaten egg.

Preheat the oven to 375°F (190°C) and lightly grease a 6-cup muffin tin. On a cutting board, lay out a sheet of phyllo pastry and brush lightly with some of the remaining ¼ cup (60 mL) olive oil. Lay a second sheet of phyllo on top and brush with more oil, and repeat with the remaining 2 sheets of phyllo on top. (See Technique.) Cut layered phyllo into 6 squares and gently press into the prepared muffin tin. Spoon cooled potato-mushroom filling into each. Slice the brie and place on top. Bake for 18 to 23 minutes, or until phyllo pastry is a rich golden brown. Serve immediately. *Makes 6 individual tarts*

FILLING
2 cups **peeled and diced Yukon Gold potatoes (½-inch/1 cm dice)** 500 mL
2 Tbsp + ¼ cup **olive oil** 30 mL + 60 mL
¾ lb **fresh shiitake mushrooms, stems removed and sliced** 375 g
1 **shallot, sliced**
1 clove **garlic, minced**
2 Tbsp **dry vermouth** 30 mL
salt & pepper
1 **large egg, beaten**

THE TARTS
4 sheets **phyllo pastry**
3 oz **single crème brie** 90 g

TASTE It's important to taste what you're cooking at the temperature it will be served. Be sure to give your potato-mushroom filling a taste while it's still warm to check for proper seasoning, since that is the temperature at which the tarts will be served.

TECHNIQUE Working with phyllo pastry doesn't have to be an agonizing process. While it's best to work quickly, don't rush so fast that you tear the pastry. I unroll the package of phyllo and cover it with a sheet of plastic wrap, then with a damp towel. The damp towel keeps the pastry from drying, but the plastic wrap prevents the moisture from the towel seeping in and gluing the layers together. If you find your pastry is tearing as you layer it, it's fine to place one or two more sheets on, for insurance.

TALE I've made these before with a triple crème brie, only to find that because of the cheese's rich and delicate nature, it melted away into nothingness! (A good, standard single crème brie works best.)

CHAMPAGNE SHRIMP ON ENDIVE

This is an elegant hors d'oeuvre that is seasonless. It suits a holiday open house, a bridal shower or a backyard soirée. Poaching the shrimp in champagne (that is, sparkling wine) adds real flair.

SHRIMP
1 bottle **(3 cups/750 mL)**
   sparkling wine, chilled
2 **lemons, sliced**
3 sprigs **fresh tarragon**
1 lb **shrimp (21/25), peeled**
   and deveined 500 g
splash **champagne vinegar**

TARRAGON
   MAYONNAISE
½ cup **mayonnaise** 125 mL
1 Tbsp **prepared horse-**
   radish 15 mL
1 Tbsp **champagne vinegar**
   15 mL
2 tsp **finely chopped fresh**
   tarragon 10 mL

FOR ASSEMBLY
3 heads **Belgian endive**
edible flowers, for garnish

For the shrimp, bring the sparkling wine, lemon slices and tarragon up to a simmer in a sauté pan. (I start with chilled sparkling wine as the bottle will open without spilling.) Add the shrimp and cook just below a simmer until pink, about 3 minutes. Remove with a slotted spoon and cool.

Remove the tails from the shrimp and slice the shrimp in half length-wise. Toss them with a splash of champagne vinegar and chill until ready to assemble.

For the tarragon mayonnaise dip, stir all the ingredients together and chill until ready to assemble.

To assemble, separate 16 endive spears and arrange on a platter. Spoon or pipe a teaspoonful (5 mL) of dip at the base of each spear. Arrange 2 shrimp halves over dip (shrimp can curl over each other). Garnish with a petal from a flower, or a single flower if small. *Serves 10 (42–50 hors d'oeuvres)*

TASTE Save the Dom Péri-gnon or Veuve Clicquot for the party, and use a basic sparkling wine for the poaching.

TECHNIQUE Because the shrimp cook so quickly and spend such a short time in the poaching liquid, it's important to peel them before cooking to give them contact time with the flavoring agents, namely the champagne, tarragon and lemon.

TALE Or in this case, "tail." It's a pet peeve of mine to order a pasta or risotto with shrimp to find the tails of the shrimp left on. Sure it makes the shrimp look bigger, but then I am left awkwardly wrestling the shrimp out of its tail, or it breaks off and I lose that tasty bit left in it.

VIETNAMESE SHRIMP SALAD ROLLS WITH PEANUT DIPPING SAUCE

Refreshing and mild, these salad rolls are perfect for an *alfresco* setting. You can prepare them up to six hours in advance, but store them tightly wrapped in a damp paper towel and plastic wrap.

½ pkg **vermicelli rice noodles**
2 Tbsp **rice vinegar** 30 mL
salt
8 leaves **green leaf lettuce**
8 **large rice paper rounds**
16 **cooked and peeled medium to large shrimp, cut in half lengthwise**
¼ cup **finely shredded carrot** 60 mL
⅓ cup **finely shredded cabbage** 80 mL

2 Tbsp **chopped unsalted peanuts** 30 mL
1 **green onion, sliced on the bias**
¼ cup **fresh basil leaves (preferably Thai basil)** 60 mL
¼ cup **fresh mint leaves** 60 mL
¼ cup **fresh cilantro leaves** 60 mL
to serve **Peanut Dipping Sauce (see facing page)**

In a bowl soak the noodles in very hot water to cover for 15 minutes. Drain well in a colander. With scissors cut the noodles into 3- to 4-inch (8 to 10 cm) lengths and in a small bowl toss with the vinegar and some salt to taste.

Cut out and discard ribs from lettuce leaves, halving each leaf.

In a shallow baking pan (a pie plate also works well) soak 1 rice paper round in hot water until pliable, under 1 minute.

Carefully spread rice paper on a tea towel and blot with paper towels. Arrange 2 pieces of lettuce on the rice paper, then 4 shrimp halves, and then the shredded carrot and cabbage over the shrimp. Spread a small handful of rice noodles over and sprinkle with peanuts and green onion. Top with basil leaves, mint and cilantro. Tightly roll up the rice paper, folding in sides when half rolled. Repeat with remaining rice paper rounds. If not serving right away, wrap rolls with a damp paper towel, then in plastic wrap (or store in a resealable bag) and chill.

To serve, slice each roll in half diagonally and serve with Peanut Dipping Sauce. *Makes 8 rolls*

PEANUT DIPPING SAUCE

3 Tbsp **pure peanut butter** 45 mL

3 Tbsp **hoisin sauce** 45 mL

1 Tbsp **sesame oil** 15 mL

1 Tbsp **tomato paste** 15 mL

3 cloves **garlic, minced**

2 tsp **finely grated fresh ginger** 10 mL

1 tsp **sugar** 5 mL

¼ tsp **chili pepper flakes** 1 mL

Bring all the ingredients with ¾ cup (190 mL) water up to a simmer in a saucepan over medium heat. Simmer, stirring occasionally, for 5 minutes.

Serve the sauce warm or at room temperature. *Makes about 1 cup (250 mL)*

TASTE While the dipping sauce is traditionally made with peanuts, any natural nut butter can be used in place of the peanut butter. And try the sauce as a dressing for a noodle salad!

TECHNIQUE Rolling the salad rolls, like anything worth doing, takes a little practice—the first one will probably be a great one for you to test (in other words, make the evidence disappear!). Our good friend Hung, who taught us how to make *pho* (page 14), also gave us a great tip for rolling salad rolls. After lightly soaking the rice paper round, he places it on a tea towel or a piece of nonslip plastic—you know, the stuff you buy in the dollar store to keep water glasses or cutting boards from slipping. This way, after arranging the fillings, you're not wrestling with the rice paper to fold and roll it neatly—it will lift away easily and not tear.

TALE At a local "wine and graze" event I catered last year, I served these rolls using local, seasonal ingredients—the event was in June, so that meant asparagus and sliced strawberries. With the basil and mint in there, it was a refreshing, heavenly snack.

EASY BRANDIED PORK TERRINE WITH CRANBERRY

When it comes to pâté, I prefer a finely textured liver pâté that I can spread on toast points. But when it comes to *terrine*, I prefer one made with richly flavored meat, not liver-based at all. I find this recipe easy to make at home, but it definitely has a restaurant quality to it, especially when served on toasted bread or with a little mustard.

In a large bowl, toss the cubed bread with the whipping cream and (unwhisked) egg whites and let sit for 30 minutes. Stir to blend; the bread should break down while stirring. Set aside.

Preheat the oven to 325°F (160°C). Soak the cranberries in brandy for 5 minutes. In a food processor, blend the pork with celery salt, black pepper, cumin, nutmeg and allspice. Add the bread mixture and blend until smooth. Add the brandy that the cranberries have been soaking in to the pork mixture, and quickly pulse. Transfer the pork mixture to a large bowl and stir in the cranberries and pistachios.

Line an 8½- x 4½-inch (1.5 L) loaf pan with parchment paper. Line the bottom and sides of the lined loaf pan with prosciutto ham so that the ham hangs off the sides of the pan. Spoon and spread the pork filling into the pan and fold the prosciutto over to cover completely, adding extra prosciutto if necessary. Place a piece of parchment over the top of pan and then cover with foil. Bake on a baking sheet for about 60 minutes, or until an internal temperature of 165°F (74°C) is reached. Cool the terrine in the loaf pan, then chill completely before turning out and slicing. *Makes one 8½- x 4½-inch (1.5 L) terrine (12 portions)*

3 cups **diced stale white bread, crusts removed (½-inch/1 cm cubes)** 750 mL

½ cup **whipping cream (35%)** 125 mL

2 **large egg whites**

½ cup **dried cranberries** 125 mL

3 Tbsp **brandy** 45 mL

1 lb **fresh ground pork** 500 g

1 Tbsp **celery salt** 15 mL

½ tsp **ground black pepper** 2 mL

¼ tsp **ground cumin** 1 mL

¼ tsp **ground nutmeg** 1 mL

¼ tsp **ground allspice** 1 mL

½ cup **shelled pistachios** 125 mL

10–12 slices **prosciutto ham**

TASTE The combination of cranberries and pistachios is very festive, making this an ideal dish to make around holiday time.

TECHNIQUE The easy-to-eat texture of a terrine is markedly different from an everyday meatloaf. This is because terrines typically contain a combination of egg whites and cream; so do many mousses and pâtés.

TALE I give full credit to Michael for this recipe. He is the master of terrines and savory mousses (salmon, shrimp, sole, etc.) and has taught me so much.

LUNCHEON SANDWICH TORTE This looks
like a dessert torte and slices like a dessert torte, but is essentially like
three styles of tea sandwich layered together.

CHICKEN SALAD

4 oz **cream cheese, at room
temperature** 120 g

½ cup **mayonnaise** 125 mL

¼ cup **chopped green onion**
60 mL

1 Tbsp **lemon juice** 15 mL

1 Tbsp **poppy seeds** 15 mL

1 tsp **sugar** 5 mL

2½ cups **finely diced cooked
chicken meat** 625 mL

⅓ cup **store-bought walnut
crumbs, lightly toasted**
80 mL

salt & pepper

EGG SALAD

8 **hard-boiled eggs, peeled**

⅔ cup **mayonnaise** 160 mL

⅓ cup **finely chopped green
olives** 80 mL

3 Tbsp **finely diced red
onion** 45 mL

salt & pepper

PESTO CREAM
CHEESE

1 cup **loosely packed fresh
basil leaves** 250 mL

⅔ cup **loosely packed fresh
Italian parsley leaves**
160 mL

2 cloves **garlic, minced**

3 Tbsp **olive oil** 45 mL

1 lb **cream cheese, at room
temperature** 500 g

2–3 Tbsp **sour cream**
30–45 mL

salt & pepper

FOR THE TORTE

1 loaf **whole wheat sandwich bread (sliced)**

1 loaf **white sandwich bread
(sliced)**

For the chicken salad, stir the cream cheese, mayonnaise, green onion,
lemon juice, poppy seeds and sugar in a bowl until blended. Add the chicken
and walnuts and season to taste. Chill until ready to assemble.

For the egg salad, grate eggs coarsely on a box grater. Toss with
the mayonnaise, olives and onion and season to taste. Chill until ready to
assemble.

For the pesto cream cheese, pulse the basil, parsley, garlic and olive oil in a food processor. Add the cream cheese and pulse to combine, adding sour cream as necessary to make it smooth. Season to taste and hold at room temperature until ready to assemble.

To assemble the torte, line a 9-inch (1.5 L) springform pan with plastic wrap so that it hangs over the sides. Remove the crusts from the sandwich bread. Cut each crustless slice of bread in half so you have 2 rectangles (about the size of ladyfingers, about 1½ inches [4 cm] wide). Line the bottom and sides of the pan with the bread slices, alternating whole wheat and white bread. Spread the chicken salad over the bread-lined bottom of the pan. Layer the bread slices over the chicken salad (alternating whole wheat and white again) and spread over the egg salad. Repeat with the bread slices and pesto cream cheese, and top with a final layer of bread slices. Cover the torte with the overhanging plastic wrap and chill for at least 3 hours.

To serve, slice as you would a cake and serve with a side salad.

Serves 8 to 10

TASTE This is one of my favorite chicken salad recipes—the cream cheese adds density but it also adds zip. (It also makes the torte slice easily.) And the addition of poppy seeds and walnuts will make it stand on its own as a regular weekday sandwich pick.

TECHNIQUE I tend to buy artisanal bread most of the time (or make it myself), but this is one instance where squishy sandwich bread does the trick. And use store-bought walnut crumbs—they are finer than walnut pieces and coarser than ground walnuts. The texture is ideal for the chicken salad to help bind it, making it easier to slice as part of the torte.

TALE I was first inspired to make this torte at the special request of regular customers of mine, Bob and Jean. It was for Bob's birthday—he doesn't eat a lot of sweets but his wife wanted him to have a birthday cake. This became it, and this torte now and again appears on our menu at the store.

SPICED LAMB & PEPPER CALZONE WITH DATES & GOAT CHEESE

The dates are a pleasant surprise in these calzones, and compared to their saucy inspirations, these are less messy to eat.

DOUGH

½ cup **tepid water (about 105°F/41°C)** 125 mL
½ tsp **instant yeast** 2 mL
¾ cup **all-purpose flour, more for rolling** 190 mL
¼ cup **pastry flour** 60 mL
½ tsp **fine salt** 2 mL

LAMB FILLING

1 Tbsp **extra virgin olive oil** 15 mL
8 oz **ground lamb** 250 g
½ cup **diced onion** 125 mL
2 cloves **garlic, minced**
1 tsp **finely grated lemon zest** 5 mL
1 tsp **ground cumin** 5 mL
1 tsp **ground coriander** 5 mL
½ tsp **ground cinnamon** 2 mL
1 cup **sliced roasted red peppers (from a jar)** 250 mL

¾ cup **tomato purée** 190 mL
8 **Medjool dates, pitted and chopped**
2 Tbsp **capers** 30 mL
salt & pepper
5 oz **fresh goat cheese, crumbled** 150 g
½ cup **chopped fresh Italian parsley** 125 mL
1 **egg whisked with 2 Tbsp (30 mL) water, for brushing**

For the dough, combine the water and yeast in a medium bowl, then stir in the 2 flours and salt. With a wooden spoon, vigorously mix dough until it just comes together, then turn the dough out onto a lightly floured work surface and knead until dough feels elastic, about 2 minutes (adding a touch more water or flour if needed—dough should be pliable and just a little sticky). Cover bowl with plastic wrap and set aside for 30 minutes.

For the lamb filling, heat the oil in a sauté pan over medium heat and add the lamb and onion. Sauté the lamb until no longer pink, and drain off excess fat. Add the garlic, lemon zest and spices and cook 1 minute more. Stir in the peppers, tomato purée, dates and capers and simmer until mixture thickens slightly, about 5 minutes, then season to taste. Let the lamb mixture cool while rolling the dough.

Preheat the oven to 375°F (190°C) and line 2 baking sheets with parchment paper.

On a lightly floured surface, turn out dough and divide into 4 (or 8) pieces. With a floured rolling pin, roll out each piece of dough into an oval as thinly as possible, about 8 inches (20 cm) long (or 4 inches/ 10 cm for the smaller calzones) and place on the baking sheets. Stir the goat cheese and parsley into the cooled lamb mixture (see Technique). Spoon the filling along the center of each. Brush the outside edge with water, fold the dough from each side over the filling and pinch the edges. Brush with the egg wash and bake for 18 to 20 minutes, or until the crust is lightly browned. Serve warm. *Serves 8 as an appetizer, 4 as an entrée*

TASTE While calzones may be Italian, these have a Moroccan twist to them. The dough is almost the same as for the Provençal Tarte (next page), so rolls thinly and easily. These calzones are all about the filling, not the dough. Extra virgin olive oil is recommended even for sautéing to compete with the strong taste of lamb.

TECHNIQUE It's important to wait until the lamb filling has cooled before stirring in the goat cheese, otherwise the cheese melts into the filling and loses its presence.

TALE This is a great way to introduce lamb to those who may not have had it before. The spices really highlight its good qualities, and here I find it a little more delicate, believe it or not, than beef.

PROVENÇAL TARTE

Sadly I have never been to Provence, but I love to read about it. I do know that the flavors of this thin-crust pizza are typical of the region. I think I'd like to visit Provence soon!

For the dough, combine the water and yeast in a medium bowl, then stir in the flours and salt. With a wooden spoon, vigorously mix dough until it just comes together, then turn dough out onto a lightly floured work surface and knead until dough feels elastic, about 2 minutes (add a touch more water or flour if needed—dough should be pliable and just a little sticky). Cover bowl with plastic wrap and set aside for 30 minutes.

For the topping, toss the tomatoes, red onion and garlic in a bowl and add red chili flakes or black pepper to taste. (Do not add salt as the other toppings will lend enough saltiness.) Stir in the olive oil.

Preheat the oven to 425°F (220°C) and line 2 baking sheets with parchment paper.

On a lightly floured surface (you can use spelt flour for rolling), turn out the dough and divide it into 4 pieces. With a floured rolling pin, roll out each piece of dough into an oval as thinly as possible, about 8 inches (20 cm) long and 5 inches (12 cm) across, and place on the baking sheets. Spoon the tomato mixture over the crust, leaving just a ½-inch (1 cm) edge, and then top with olives, capers and anchovies. Bake tartes for 12 to 15 minutes on the lower rack of the oven, until the edges of the dough are lightly browned. While still warm, sprinkle with whole basil leaves. Drizzle lightly with olive oil and serve. *Makes 4 tartes • Serves 4 as an appetizer, 2 as an entrée*

DOUGH

½ cup **tepid water (about 105°F/41°C)** 125 mL
½ tsp **instant yeast** 2 mL
½ cup **spelt flour** 125 mL
½ cup **all-purpose flour, more for rolling** 125 mL
½ tsp **fine salt** 2 mL

TOPPING

1 pint **grape tomatoes, cut in half** 500 mL
¼ **red onion, thinly sliced**
2 cloves **garlic, minced**
red chili flakes or ground black pepper
2 Tbsp **extra virgin olive oil, plus extra for drizzling** 30 mL
½ cup **pitted niçoise olives** 125 mL
2 Tbsp **capers** 30 mL
16 **anchovy fillets**
½ cup **loosely packed fresh basil leaves** 125 mL

TASTE This tarte makes a great hors d'oeuvre, sliced into small pieces. The salty kick of capers, anchovy and olives whet the appetite and make a perfect patio partner to a glass of rosé. Using spelt flour lends an earthy flavor that works well with the intensely flavored toppings, and its lower gluten content helps to produce a crispy crust.

TECHNIQUE This pizza dough is a quick-rise recipe, so you don't have to wait for it too long. One of the keys to a tender thin crust, though, is in resting the dough. If you are rolling the dough and it springs back on you, just set it aside for five minutes, then come back to it—it will yield and roll quite thinly.

TALE I am honestly fascinated by Provence and all things Provençal. I think I've held off on traveling there only because I've painted such a bright, sunny picture of the place, full of such lively tastes and personalities, that I fear I might be disappointed when I finally do visit.

[FISH & SEAFOOD]

Fish offers such a variety of taste and texture. When you think about it, beef is, well, just beef. You can use different cuts, marinate it, change up your cooking method and serve it with any number of sauces, but it's still beef.

Fish, on the other hand, offers diversity before you even consider marinating, cooking or adding sauces. Freshwater versus saltwater fish, cold water versus warm water fish, large versus small. There are so many textures and flavors that it's no wonder that sometimes just grilling fish and serving it with lemon sounds appealing—and often it's the tastiest option.

But like everything, sometimes we want something a little bit more complex, and if providing some spectacular recipes for fish dishes makes us visit the seafood counter more often, then that's what has to be done.

If you don't already, it's time to start asking questions to the person behind the fish counter (who can hopefully give you answers): Where does the fish come from? Is it fresh or previously frozen? (Although, fresh does not always equal better . . . Fish is flash-frozen on the ship for safer transportation and can arrive in better shape than fresh, sometimes.) Is it farmed or wild? Line caught or net? There is so much information out there that this little introduction cannot do it justice, but I know you can draw parameters and design preferences of your own.

BAJA FISH TACOS
Ground meat or sliced chicken is the most common taco filling, but diced fish, marinated and quickly sautéed, makes a refreshing change, and it takes a fraction of the time to cook compared to beef or chicken.

1 lb **medium to firm white fish, such as marlin, shark, haddock or cod** 500 g

1 clove **garlic, minced**

2 Tbsp **lime juice** 30 mL

1 Tbsp **olive oil** 15 mL

1 **jalapeño pepper, seeded and minced**

3 Tbsp **finely chopped red onion** 45 mL

salt & pepper

FOR ASSEMBLY

8 **soft flour tortillas**

2 cups **shredded red cabbage** 500 mL

1 cup **diced fresh tomato** 250 mL

1 cup **diced avocado** 250 mL

½ cup **sour cream** 125 mL

¼ cup **chopped fresh cilantro** 60 mL

hot sauce (optional)

Cut the fish into 1-inch (2.5 cm) cubes and toss with the garlic, lime juice, olive oil and jalapeño. Cover and chill for 20 minutes. While fish is marinating, prepare the other ingredients for assembly, placing the vegetables, sour cream and cilantro in individual bowls. Put on the serving table.

Heat a sauté pan over medium-high heat. Add the marinated fish and sauté until cooked through, about 5 minutes. Remove from the heat, stir in the red onion and season to taste. Transfer to a serving dish.

To serve, let everyone spoon fish into a soft tortilla and top with remaining ingredients. *Serves 4*

TASTE A firm fish takes on marinating very nicely. However, don't marinate it for too long, otherwise the lime juice will actually penetrate the fish and "cook" it.

TECHNIQUE With assemble-your-own dishes such as this one, color is key when choosing the toppings. The red cabbage stands out on a platter (and adds great crunch), while the red and green of tomato and avocado complement each other nicely. Of course, this is also one of the dishes that have no rules—use whatever toppings you like best.

TALE Michael and I enjoyed our first fish tacos in Mexico on vacation. They were made with marlin, and we loved the texture of the firm fish with the spicy salsa and fresh, crunchy toppings—*muis bueno*!

CHOWDER FISH CAKES
These fish cakes can be served as is beside a nice salad, or put on a bun and topped with a little tartar sauce or Garlic Dressing (page 39).

4 slices **bacon, diced**
½ cup **finely diced onion** 125 mL
½ cup **finely diced red bell pepper** 125 mL
⅓ cup **finely diced celery** 80 mL
1 tsp **chopped fresh thyme** 5 mL
½ tsp **celery salt** 2 mL
¼ tsp **paprika** 1 mL

2½ cups **peeled and diced Yukon Gold potato, cut into ½-inch (1 cm) pieces** 625 mL
¾ lb **cooked fish, such as salmon or cod** 375 g
1 cup **fresh or frozen corn** 250 mL
salt & pepper
3 **eggs**
¾ cup **dry breadcrumbs** 190 mL
2 Tbsp **olive oil** 30 mL

In a sauté pan over medium heat, cook the bacon until crisp. Remove the bacon and reserve. Add the onion, red pepper, celery, thyme, celery salt and paprika to the pan with the bacon drippings, cooking until onions are translucent. While sautéing the vegetables, boil the potatoes in salted water until tender, about 15 minutes, and drain. Let the potatoes cool for 10 minutes, place in a bowl and roughly mash with a fork.

Add the sautéed vegetables to the cooled potatoes and then flake in the fish. Stir in the corn and reserved bacon, and season to taste. Break 1 egg into a small dish, whisk with a fork and add to the potato mixture, stirring the mixture well. Shape into 12 balls and press to flatten into patties.

Whisk the remaining 2 eggs and place breadcrumbs in a separate bowl. Dip each fish cake in egg to coat completely, then dip into bread-crumbs. To cook, heat the olive oil in a sauté pan over medium-high heat. Place fish cakes in pan and cook about 6 minutes on each side, turning carefully.

Serve fish cakes as is or on a bun with tartar sauce and lemon.

Makes 12 fish cakes

TASTE I always add fresh thyme to my chowder (and as you can tell from the title I think of this recipe as a chowder in fish cake form—see Technique). I find that thyme highlights all the other flavors and harmonizes the dish.

TECHNIQUE A chowder contains bacon, potato and a milk base thickened with flour, and seafood chowders are the most common. Of course, I skipped on the milk here because I sure didn't want soggy fish cakes!

TALE I've made miniature versions of these fish cakes and served them as hot hors d'oeuvres. Switch the fish with crab and you've got fabulous crab cakes.

BAKED COD WITH GARLIC ALMOND SAUCE

I love the flaky texture and mild flavor of cod, which, next to haddock, is my choice for fish and chips. But it's also delicious baked and served with this creamy garlic sauce, which is thickened with ground almonds and served at room temperature. This dish is fantastic served any time of year.

Stir the ground almonds, milk and 1 cup (250 mL) water together and chill for at least 6 hours or overnight.

Slice the garlic and place in a small bowl. Pour boiling water to cover. Let sit for 15 minutes, then drain. (This blanches the garlic to take the edge off.)

In a food processor, blend the garlic with the almond mixture, breadcrumbs and vinegar until smooth. With the machine running, pour in the olive oil in a thin stream. Adjust the thickness to sauce consistency with water, if necessary. Season to taste and keep in the fridge if making this beforehand, but bring it back to room temperature when ready to serve.

For the cod, preheat the oven to 400°F (200°C) and line a baking sheet with parchment paper. Place the cod portions on the baking sheet and brush with olive oil. Season lightly and bake for 12 to 15 minutes, or until fish flakes when touched with a fork.

To serve, spoon the sauce on each plate and place the cod portion on top. Finish with a few drops of balsamic vinegar and serve. *Serves 6*

SAUCE

1 cup **ground almonds** 250 mL
⅓ cup **2% milk** 80 mL
3 cloves **garlic**
½ cup **dry breadcrumbs** 125 mL
1 Tbsp **sherry vinegar** 15 mL
½ cup **extra virgin olive oil, plus extra for fish** 125 mL
salt & pepper

6 **portions of fresh cod, about 6 oz (175 g) each**
salt & pepper
balsamic vinegar, for garnish

TASTE The trick of blanching the garlic in hot water is a great one when you want to use it raw (such as in this sauce, or in salsa) but want to take the "edge" off it. It works well and you won't be haunted by garlic breath nearly as much.

TECHNIQUE This sauce is thickened by two things—the ground almonds, which absorb the milk as they sit, and the olive oil, which emulsifies (or binds) all the ingredients together. I love using the full ½ cup (125 mL) measure of olive oil, but you can reduce the amount to ¼ cup (60 mL) if you wish. Don't eliminate it completely, however—the sauce would suffer, both taste- and texture-wise.

TALE The sauce is inspired by a classic Spanish soup—essentially made the same way but with more milk. It's a refreshing start to a summer meal, but I like the seasonless character of it, a sauce to be served any time of year.

BISTRO SKATE WING WITH CAPERS & BROWN BUTTER

I love French bistro food, and this is one of the dishes I crave now and again. Skate is a kind of ray, and is made up mostly of cartilage. The wings have meat on two sides, but like sole and flounder, one side has more than the other.

To prepare the skate wing, put some flour on a plate. Dredge each skate wing with the flour and shake off the excess. Season each side and set on a plate.

Preheat the oven to 200°F (95°C). Heat a large sauté pan over high heat and add 2 Tbsp (30 mL) butter. Wait until the butter foams and subsides before adding 2 skate wings. (The butter will brown a bit—see Technique.) Sear until you can pull away the skate from the bone with a fork, about 8 minutes. Turn over and sear the other side. Transfer to a plate and keep warm in the oven. Add 2 more Tbsp (30 mL) of butter, let the foam subside then repeat with remaining 2 skate wings.

To make the sauce, add the capers to the sauté pan over high heat and stir to heat. Squeeze in the juice of half a lemon. Reduce heat to low and add remaining 2 Tbsp (30 mL) butter, stirring until melted. Season to taste and spoon over skate wing portions. Serve with lemon wedges.

Serves 4

4 **small skate wings, about 12 oz (375 g) each**
flour, for dredging
salt & pepper
6 Tbsp **butter, divided** 90 mL
⅓ cup **capers** 80 mL
1 **lemon, one-half cut into wedges for serving**

TASTE Fresh skate wing tastes a bit like scallop, and the meat has a lovely texture that easily pulls away from the thick bone in the center. Skate wing is best purchased very fresh. Ask to see it up close when ordering at the fish counter. If the skate has even the faintest ammonia nose to it, pass on it and wait until the next delivery.

TECHNIQUE Cooking in brown butter adds depth of flavor to the simplest dishes. By cooking the butter until it stops foaming and starts taking on color, you are actually caramelizing the milk solids in it.

TALE Confession time. Yes, I've included this recipe because it is one of my favorites—but it's actually Michael who makes it for me most of the time.

HALIBUT IN PARCHMENT WITH WHITE BALSAMIC & SHIITAKE MUSHROOMS

Halibut is all about the texture. It's meaty yet flaky, and also mild yet with its own fresh taste. Halibut's best qualities shine through when it is baked in parchment, as the fish is essentially steamed. The aromatics of shiitake, thyme, bay leaf and sesame oil just serve to accentuate the fish and make it a perfect entrée when entertaining guests.

4 **halibut fillets, skins removed**, about 5 oz (150 g) each	4 **fresh or dry bay leaves**
2 **shallots**	4 tsp **white balsamic vinegar or champagne vinegar** 20 mL
½ lb **shiitake mushrooms** 220 g	4 tsp **extra virgin olive oil** 20 mL
parchment paper	1 tsp **sesame oil** 5 mL
4 sprigs **fresh thyme**	**salt & pepper**

Preheat the oven to 375°F (190°C).

Rinse the halibut portions and pat dry. Slice the shallots. Remove the stems from the shiitake mushrooms and slice. Cut 4 sheets of parchment paper, 12 x 16 inches (30 x 40 cm) each.

To assemble, fold the parchment paper in half to create a crease. Open the parchment flat and sprinkle a few shallots on 1 side of the fold of each sheet. Place a halibut portion on the shallots and top with mushrooms. Lay a spring of thyme and a bay leaf on each and drizzle with white balsamic (or champagne vinegar), olive oil and a few drops of sesame oil. Season each lightly.

Fold over the parchment and seal the packages by making a series of small folds starting from one of the folded corners to create a half-moon shape (see Technique). Place the parcels on a baking sheet and bake until parcels puff up, about 18 minutes. To serve, transfer entire parcels to individual plates. Each guest should tear open the parcel to expose the fragrance (and also remove the thyme and bay leaf before eating). *Serves 4*

TASTE The earthiness of the shiitake mushrooms along with the sesame oil add, for lack of a better term, a masculine edge to a delicate dish. By steaming everything, though, the flavor is balanced, and it all works.

TECHNIQUE Making parchment folds to create a good seal is important. The first few folds are the toughest, as they are the ones that get you going. Make sure those first few folds completely fold over the last, so that no actual edges of the parchment paper are visible. After the last fold, be sure to give the paper a good twist—this will secure all the folds.

TALE It's just so impressive to serve these parchment parcels at a dinner party. As each guest tears open their "gift," the fragrance will waft out and fill the dining room. Everyone can eat directly out of the parchment parcel, or you can pass around an empty platter for guests to place their paper onto for disposal.

PHOTO Halibut in Parchment *served with* Asparagus with Avocado Wasabi "Butter" (page 149)

UPBEAT COQUILLE ST. JACQUES

This is a more up-to-date version of scallops baked in a creamy sauce, except, unlike the '70s version, you don't need to serve it in a scallop shell or coquille dish, nor do you pipe an edge of mashed potatoes around the outside. You'll be impressed by how simple yet decadent this dish is. It could also make a great appetizer for eight people.

¾ cup **sour cream (14% M.F., not low fat)** 190 mL

½ cup **mayonnaise** 125 mL

1 cup + 2 Tbsp **finely grated Parmesan cheese** 250 mL + 30 mL

3 Tbsp **lemon juice** 45 mL

ground black pepper

1¼ lb **bay scallops** 625 g

2 Tbsp **dry breadcrumbs** 30 mL

2 Tbsp **finely chopped green onion or chives** 30 mL

Preheat the oven to 425°F (220°C). Stir sour cream, mayonnaise, 1 cup (250 mL) Parmesan, lemon juice and black pepper (no salt is necessary). Rinse scallops, pat dry and stir into mayonnaise mixture. Spread into a 4-cup (1 L) baking dish. Stir the breadcrumbs and remaining 2 Tbsp (30 mL) Parmesan to combine and sprinkle on top. Bake for 15 to 18 minutes, or until the edges of the dish are bubbling. Garnish with the chopped green onion and serve immediately. *Serves 4*

TASTE Typically cheese and fish (or seafood) do not go well together, unless it's a mild, fresh cheese such as ricotta, chèvre or mascarpone. Cheese usually makes fish or seafood taste stronger, or "off." But sometimes something just works even though it breaks the rules. In this case, the Parmesan makes the scallops taste sweeter.

TECHNIQUE This dish is a variation of what we often do with large sea scallops. We start off with a smaller amount of the sour cream mixture (with more Parmesan to make it a bit thicker) and spoon it onto individual sea scallops. Then we broil the scallops so the Parmesan topping browns and bubbles while the scallops just cook through. It makes a great hors d'oeuvre at holiday time, as we can attest to almost every holiday. It was Michael's sister, Linda, who showed us this trick.

TALE My first taste of Coquille St. Jacques was at a fancy family dinner at the Oban Inn in Niagara-on-the-Lake, long before I moved to this area. It was my first taste of scallops, and I had never seen anything so elegant as lunch served in a real seashell.

SOLE PAUPIETTE

Not to be confused with *en papillote*, or "in paper" (like Halibut in Parchment, page 80), *paupiette* simply refers to a thin piece of fish or meat wrapped around a filling. By spreading an herbed filling on the sole fillets and then rolling them, you keep the fish moist and flavorful at the same time.

FILLING
½ cup **dry breadcrumbs** 125 mL

3 Tbsp **finely chopped green onion** 45 mL

1 Tbsp **chopped fresh tarragon** 15 mL

2 tsp **chopped fresh oregano or marjoram** 10 mL

1 tsp **chopped fresh thyme** 5 mL

1 tsp **finely grated lemon zest** 5 mL

2 Tbsp **melted butter** 30 mL

½ tsp **fine salt** 2 mL

¼ tsp **ground black pepper** 1 mL

FILLETS
1½ lb **sole fillets (1 or 2 per person, depending on size)** 750 g

2 **shallots**

1 cup **dry white wine** 250 mL

2 Tbsp **butter** 30 mL

Preheat the oven to 375°F (190°C). For the filling, stir all the ingredients together—the mixture should be moist but still crumbly.

If the sole fillets are large, split them in half lengthwise down the center. Spread a spoonful of filling over the top each fillet. Roll up the fillets, making a pinwheel of sorts. Place the rolled fillets in a lightly greased baking dish.

Slice the shallots and place in a small saucepan with the wine. Bring up to a simmer and reduce by half. Stir in the butter to melt, and pour the sauce over the sole. Cover the dish with foil and bake for 18 to 20 minutes, or until the fish flakes when touched with a fork. Serve immediately. *Serves 6*

TASTE Sole is just about the mildest fish you can buy, so it's a good choice if you are introducing fish to kids for the first time (but maybe without the white wine sauce!).

TECHNIQUE The fish is baked, but the cooking method of this dish is more of a poach or braise. The white wine that the sole cooks in is so nice spooned over the paupiettes as a sauce.

TALE I've also used the same filling as a herbed breadcrumb crust on top of baked salmon—it browns nicely and keeps in the moisture of the fish.

SHERRY SEAFOOD BAKE

This easy-to-make dish is sort of like a Tuesday-night version of seafood bisque. It's not nearly as rich as bisque though, and it's more than just a first course—it's definitely an entrée.

3 Tbsp + 2 Tbsp **butter** 45 mL + 30 mL

1 cup **finely diced onion** 250 mL

½ cup **finely diced celery** 125 mL

2 cloves **garlic, minced**

1 tsp **chopped fresh thyme** 5 mL

3 Tbsp **all-purpose flour** 45 mL

2 cups **2% milk** 500 mL

½ tsp **dry mustard** 2 mL

⅓ cup **finely chopped sun-dried tomato** 80 mL

1 lb **small shrimp (51/60), peeled, deveined and tails removed** 500 g

1 lb **bay scallops** 500 g **OR** ½ lb **crabmeat** 250 g

3 Tbsp **sherry** 45 mL

½ tsp **fine salt** 2 mL

¼ tsp **ground black or white pepper** 1 mL

⅓ cup **chopped fresh Italian parsley** 80 mL

⅓ cup **dry breadcrumbs** 80 mL

Melt 3 Tbsp (45 mL) of the butter in a medium saucepan over medium heat and add the onion and celery. Sauté until onions are translucent, about 5 minutes. Add the garlic and thyme and sauté 1 minute more. Add the flour and stir to coat, cooking for 3 minutes, reducing the heat if flour begins to stick. Add ½ cup (125 mL) milk and stir vigorously to create a paste. Switch to a whisk and slowly whisk in the remaining milk in 3 additions. Whisk in the mustard and bring up to a simmer. Stir in the sun-dried tomato and continue to simmer.

Preheat the oven to 375°F (190°C). Stir in the shrimp and scallops (or crabmeat), sherry and salt, pepper and parsley and bring to just below a simmer. Transfer the seafood mixture to a baking dish. In a small pot or in the microwave melt the remaining 2 Tbsp (30 mL) butter and stir into the breadcrumbs. Sprinkle breadcrumbs on top of the seafood, and bake, uncovered, for 25 minutes, or until bubbling around the edges. Cool for 10 minutes before serving. *Serves 4*

TASTE The sherry in this recipe is what distinguishes this recipe, giving it its "classic" status. A dry sherry is one of my pantry staples—I use it often when I caramelize onions and in turkey gravy to build flavor and fragrance.

TECHNIQUE If you are using frozen shrimp, scallops or crabmeat, make sure it is all completely thawed and well drained before adding to the bake. Frozen seafood will let out all its water and you'll end up with a watery, thin-tasting sauce. For proper thawing, place the package in a bowl and slowly run cold water over it until thawed, or thaw overnight in a bowl in the fridge.

TALE I call for a little dry mustard in this recipe to give it a nice flavor, but in the days before efficient refrigeration, mustard was used in sauces with seafood to mask the ammonia odors of fish that had a little "maturity" to it. A classic tip I'm glad we don't need to use anymore!

SESAME SALMON WITH ROASTED RED PEPPER SALSA

I actually like to make this dish in winter, when I crave a little color on my plate. The pepper salsa replaces a tomato salsa, which in winter is hard to make taste anything like its summertime version made with ripe tomatoes.

RED PEPPER SALSA
1 jar (12 oz/335 mL) roasted red peppers, drained
1 cup diced English cucumber 250 mL
½ cup finely diced red onion 125 mL
2 Tbsp rice wine vinegar 30 mL
1 tsp sugar 5 mL
salt & pepper
2 Tbsp chopped fresh cilantro 30 mL
1 Tbsp chopped fresh mint 15 mL
2 tsp sesame oil 10 mL

SESAME SALMON
2 Tbsp olive oil 30 mL
6 Tbsp sesame seeds 90 mL
salt & pepper
6 salmon fillets, skin on, about 6 oz (175 g) each

For the salsa, finely dice the roasted red peppers and toss with cucumber, red onion, rice wine vinegar and sugar in a bowl and season lightly. Cover and chill for 30 minutes. Drain off any excess liquid and then stir in the cilantro, mint and sesame oil. Season to taste and chill until ready to serve.

For the salmon, preheat the oven to 400°F (200°C). Pour the sesame seeds onto a plate and season lightly, stirring to mix. Heat a large, ovenproof sauté pan over medium-high heat and add the olive oil. Dip the skinless side of each salmon portion in sesame seeds and place sesame-seed side down into the hot pan. Cook for 2 minutes, then flip the salmon portions over. Immediately place the pan in the oven and cook for 10 to 15 minutes (10 for medium, 15 for well done). Serve with salsa on the side. *Serves 6*

TASTE The sesame seeds and sesame oil add a subtle Asian taste to this dish, but with all the other ingredients at play, it really can't be categorized.

TECHNIQUE Always check your salmon for pinbones, which are thin bones embedded down the center of a salmon fillet. Most salmon is sold with pinbones removed, but often a few are missed, especially at the head of the fillet. Run you fingers back and forth across the thickest part of the salmon. If you feel a bone, a pair of small needle-nose pliers takes care of them.

TALE My mom is the source of this recipe. This is her favorite way to cook salmon, and she likes how it works out for her every time, and goes with lots of other accompaniments too.

PHOTO Sesame Salmon with
Roasted Red Pepper Salsa *served
with* Braised Edamame with Leeks
& Miso (page 144)

[POULTRY]

Fish is slowly coming up in the ranks, but chicken remains the most popular protein these days. Turkey has spread its wings (ha ha, even if turkeys can't fly!) and finds itself on the dinner table beyond the holidays.

Chicken is always the easiest choice for supper, but it's also the protein that, when it comes to creating new dishes, seems to elude us. Too often we fall back on the old favorites, the dishes we can make with our eyes closed.

I've got some new ideas and fresh takes on poultry, though, so it doesn't have to be the "fallback" meal. It can be new, exciting and dare I say even adventurous?

COQ AU VIN

This dish has definitely improved over time. That is, we no longer need to tenderize a rooster (*coq au vin*), but still, marinating and cooking chicken in red wine certainly does wonders.

1 **large onion, sliced**
2 stalks **celery, sliced**
2 **carrots, peeled and sliced**
5 cloves **garlic, sliced**
1 **whole chicken, about 5 lb (2.2 kg) cut into pieces**
1 bottle **red wine, such as Cabernet Sauvignon or Syrah (3 cups/750 mL)**
4 slices **thick bacon, sliced**

¼ cup **all-purpose flour** 60 mL
1 cup **chicken stock (see page 5)** 250 mL
2 **bay leaves**
2 sprigs **fresh thyme**
1 cup **peeled pearl onions, or sweet pickled pearl onions, rinsed (see Technique)** 250 mL

salt & pepper
1 Tbsp **butter** 15 mL
4 cups **sliced button or cremini mushrooms** 1 L
¼ cup **chopped fresh Italian parsley** 60 mL

Spread the onion, celery, carrots and garlic in a large glass or earthenware dish. Arrange the chicken pieces over the vegetables and pour wine over to cover. Cover and chill for at least 6 hours, or overnight.

Remove the chicken pieces to a plate and pat dry. Strain the vegetables from the wine, reserving both separately.

Preheat the oven to 350°F (180°C). Heat a large, heavy-bottomed pot (an ovenproof Dutch oven is preferred) over medium-high heat and sauté bacon until crisp. Remove the bacon and reserve. Strain off all but 3 Tbsp (45 mL) of the bacon drippings. Sear the chicken in batches in remaining bacon fat, removing once the outside is browned, about 4 minutes per side. Reduce the heat to medium and add the reserved vegetables, sautéing until the onions are tender, about 5 minutes. Stir in the flour and cook for 3 minutes. Slowly whisk in the chicken stock and reserved wine and bring up to a simmer with the bay leaves, thyme and pearl onions. Return the chicken to the pot, season lightly, cover and place in oven. (If you aren't using an ovenproof pot, transfer to a large baking dish or roasting pan and cover tightly with foil.) Cook until chicken is tender, about 60 to 75 minutes. Remove from the oven and skim off any fat.

Add the butter to a medium sauté pan over high heat. Sauté the mushrooms, cooking until tender, about 5 minutes. Stir in the reserved bacon and season to taste, taking it off the heat.

To serve, taste the wine sauce and adjust the seasoning, then place Coq au Vin onto a large platter. Spoon bacon-mushroom mixture over and garnish with chopped parsley. *Serves 4*

TASTE I know here I'm supposed to comment on the flavor characteristics of the dish, but in this case, it's the aroma I must remark upon. Oh, the smell of onions and garlic and chicken and red wine all intermingling and wafting through the house!

TECHNIQUE To make coq au vin authentic, it should have bacon (fine), mushrooms (no problem), red wine (naturally) and pearl onions (—ugh!). I hate peeling pearl onions, and, while I know a good trick— soaking them in cool water for an hour and then peeling them while still in the water—I find that opening a jar of sweet pickled pearl onions far easier, and the subtle sweetness rounds out the dish nicely.

TALE While I believe it is more traditional to serve coq au vin with potatoes, I prefer it with buttered wide egg noodles.

CHICKEN POT PIE

A good chicken pot pie should be packed with meat and veggies, like a hearty chicken stew in a pie shell. Often I make chicken stew and serve biscuits alongside it, and that gave me the idea of baking biscuits right on top of the filling, in place of a second crust.

BOTTOM CRUST

1¼ cups **all-purpose flour** 310 mL

¼ tsp **fine salt** 1 mL

¼ cup **unsalted butter** 60 mL

¼ cup **vegetable shortening** 60 mL

1 **large egg**

1 Tbsp **lemon juice** 15 mL

1–3 Tbsp **cold water** 15–45 mL

FILLING

2 lb **boneless, skinless chicken breasts and/or chicken thighs** 1 kg

3 Tbsp **butter, divided** 45 mL

2 Tbsp **vegetable oil, divided** 30 mL

1 cup **diced onion** 250 mL

1 cup **peeled and diced carrot** 250 mL

¾ cup **peeled and diced parsnip** 190 mL

½ cup **diced celery** 125 mL

1 cup **seeded and diced red bell pepper** 250 mL

1 cup **green beans, cut into 1-inch (2.5 cm) pieces** 250 mL

¼ cup **all-purpose flour** 60 mL

2 cups **chicken stock (see page 3)** 500 mL

1 tsp **dry mustard** 5 mL

2 **bay leaves**

2 tsp **chopped fresh rosemary** 10 mL

salt & pepper

2 cups **cremini mushrooms, quartered** 500 mL

splash **dry vermouth**

[ingredients continued next page . . .]

For the crust, combine the flour with the salt. Cut in the butter and shortening using a pastry blender until the mixture is roughly even and crumbly. Whisk the egg, lemon juice and 1 Tbsp (15 mL) of cold water, then add to the flour and blend just until the dough comes together, adding remaining water if needed, a tablespoonful (15 mL) at a time, to bring dough together. Shape into a disc, wrap and chill for 30 minutes.

For the filling, dice the chicken into 1-inch (2.5 cm) pieces. Heat a large heavy-bottomed sauté pan over medium-high heat with 1 Tbsp (15 mL) each of butter and oil. Add the chicken and sauté until all sides are lightly browned, about 4 minutes per side. Remove and reduce the heat to medium. Add 1 Tbsp (15 mL) each of butter and oil and add the onion, carrot, parsnip and celery. Sauté for 3 minutes, then add the bell pepper and green beans, sautéing 3 minutes more. Add the flour and stir to coat vegetables, cooking for about 5 minutes (reduce heat if flour begins to stick). Add ½ cup (125 mL) chicken stock and stir until flour absorbs, then add remaining stock ½ cup (125 mL) at a time. Add mustard, bay leaves and rosemary, and bring up to a simmer over medium heat. Season lightly. Add the chicken and lower the heat to gently simmer, loosely covered, until chicken is fully cooked, about 20 minutes.

[continued next page . . .]

In another sauté pan over medium-high heat, melt the remaining 1 Tbsp (15 mL) butter. Add the mushrooms and sauté until all the liquid from the mushrooms has evaporated and mushrooms are tender, about 5 minutes. Add the vermouth and simmer until liquid has evaporated. Once the chicken is cooked, stir in the sautéed mushrooms and season to taste. Cool filling to room temperature. (The filling can be made in advance and chilled.)

For the cheddar biscuit topping, blend the flour, baking powder and salt to combine using a whisk (or a food processor). Cut in the pieces of butter and cheddar until the mixture is rough and crumbly. Add the milk and combine just until dough comes together. Chill in the bowl until ready to assemble.

To assemble, preheat the oven to 400°F (200°C). On a lightly floured surface, roll out the pie dough to a circle just less than ¼-inch (6 mm) thick and line a 9-inch (23 cm) pie plate or six individual 8 oz (250 mL) baking dishes that has been lightly dusted with flour. Trim the edges of the shell and spoon in the cooled filling. Break the biscuit dough into pieces overtop the filling. Place the pot pie on a baking sheet and bake for 15 minutes. Reduce the heat to 375°F (190°C) and bake until the biscuit topping is cooked through (test by pulling apart gently with a knife), about 40 more minutes.

Chicken Pot Pie can be baked in advance, cooled to room temperature, chilled and reheated for 30 minutes in a 325°F (160°C) oven.

Makes one 9-inch (23 cm) pie or six individual 8 oz (250 mL) dishes • Serves 6 to 8

CHEDDAR BISCUIT TOPPING

1½ cups **all-purpose flour** 375 mL

2 tsp **baking powder** 10 mL

½ tsp **fine salt** 2 mL

½ cup **cold unsalted butter, in pieces** 125 mL

1½ cups **grated medium cheddar cheese** 375 mL

½ cup **2% milk** 125 mL

TASTE I pack so much chicken and so many veggies into this recipe that it has no room for diced potato, typical of a pot pie. But considering that there's a pie crust at the bottom and a biscuit topping, I don't think anyone will miss the potatoes.

TECHNIQUE I find it a smart move to cook the mushrooms separately from the rest of the filling. They can sometimes impart a gray color to the filling that is not appealing.

TALE Chicken pot pie is to savory cooking as lemon meringue pie is to desserts. Both are popular dishes, yet it does take a certain time commitment to make what with the crust, the filling and the topping, and time required in between to let components cool. If you have the time, then I say, yes, it's worth the effort.

CHICKEN PUTTANESCA
This is a popular dish around the globe, as popular as the profession it's named after (uh, the oldest profession in the world, in fact)—although why it was named after this is up for debate. Regardless, puttanesca sauce is strong and punchy, and this particular preparation is great served over short pasta like penne or farfalle.

4 Tbsp **olive oil, divided** 60 mL

8 **skinless chicken thighs (bone-in or boneless)**

3 Tbsp **finely diced red onion** 45 mL

2 cloves **garlic, minced**

4 **anchovy fillets OR** 1½ Tbsp **anchovy paste** 23 mL

2 cups **diced fresh, ripe tomato (seeded)** 500 mL

½ cup **caperberries (see Technique), stems removed and cut in half** 125 mL **OR** ¼ cup **capers, drained** 60 mL

½ cup **kalamata olives, pitted and roughly chopped** 125 mL

red chili flakes

salt (optional)

1 **small bunch fresh basil**

Heat 2 Tbsp (30 mL) oil in a sauté pan over medium-high heat. Sear half the chicken thighs until browned, turning once, and remove. Repeat with the remaining chicken thighs. Reduce heat to medium and add the onion, garlic and anchovies (or paste), stirring once. Immediately add the tomato and ⅔ cup (160 mL) water and bring up to a simmer. Add the chicken to the pan and simmer uncovered until cooked through, about 30 minutes. Turn once during cooking. Remove the chicken onto a serving platter. Stir in the caperberries, olives and chili flakes and taste, adding salt if needed. Spoon the sauce over the chicken and tear basil overtop before serving. *Serves 4*

TASTE I love the salty kick of anchovies, caperberries and olives together. If anchovies aren't your thing, then extra caperberries and olives will suffice.

TECHNIQUE Caperberries can usually be found in specialty food stores, and they are like a regular caper but are the size of an olive and can be used just about anywhere a traditional caper would be used (and is also a smart garnish for a martini). If you can't locate them, regular capers will do just as satisfactorily in this recipe.

TALE All right, I've just realized as I write these final notes that I've utilized chicken *thighs* in this recipe. Lay off the puttanesca jokes, if just for a moment. Many thanks.

ROCKWELL BAKE

This turkey dish is, in essence, a *strata*—a savory bread pudding. This one contains all the elements of holiday turkey dinner—turkey breast, cranberry and stuffing with a little cheese to take it to the next level. It is an easy, slice-and-serve entrée that reheats just as well as holiday leftovers.

2 Tbsp **olive oil** 30 mL
1 cup **finely diced onion** 250 mL
1 cup **finely diced celery (including leaves)** 250 mL
½ cup **finely diced carrot** 125 mL
1 clove **garlic, minced**
1 Tbsp **finely chopped fresh sage** 15 mL
2 tsp **finely chopped fresh thyme** 10 mL
1 cup **dried cranberries** 250 mL
¼ cup **dry vermouth or water** 60 mL

5 **large eggs**
3 cups **2% milk** 750 mL
1 tsp **Dijon mustard** 5 mL
1½ tsp **fine salt** 7.5 mL
¼ tsp **ground black pepper** 1 mL
8 cups **diced day-old bread (white, whole wheat or mix) (1-inch/2.5 cm cubes)** 2 L
3 cups **diced cooked turkey meat (½-inch/1 cm cubes)** 750 mL
2½ cups **grated Swiss cheese** 625 mL

Preheat the oven to 350°F (180°C). Grease a 9-inch (2.5 L) springform pan and place on a baking sheet.

In a sauté pan over medium heat, add the oil and heat for a minute, then add the onion, celery and carrot. Sauté until the onions are translucent, about 5 minutes. Add the garlic and herbs, and sauté 1 minute more. Add the cranberries and vermouth or water, then simmer until almost all liquid has evaporated. Remove from heat and cool to room temperature.

While the vegetables are cooling, whisk the eggs to blend in a large bowl, then whisk in milk, mustard, salt and pepper. Add bread cubes, toss to coat and let soak for 15 minutes, stirring occasionally.

Stir the cooled vegetables and diced turkey into the bread mixture, then stir in 2 cups (500 mL) of Swiss cheese. Spoon mixture into the prepared springform pan and sprinkle with remaining ½ cup (125 mL) Swiss cheese. Bake for 60 minutes, or until the top is a rich golden brown and the center springs back when pressed. Let rest for 15 minutes before unmolding and serving. *Serves 6 to 8*

TASTE There is something exceptionally comforting about this combination of flavors. It's not just because it tastes of the holidays, but that its flavor and texture make it interesting enough without being overly challenging. Does that make sense? Maybe the turkey narcosis is kicking in.

TECHNIQUE Use the same bread, egg and milk ratio to create your own "bake." How about roast beef, horseradish, broccoli and cheddar for a "Sunday Supper Bake," or diced cooked potato with bacon, cheddar, green onion and cream cheese for a "Loaded Baked Potato Bake"? What counts is that all of the ingredients going into the bake are fully cooked.

TALE I named this dish in tribute to Norman Rockwell and his famous painting of the holiday dinner, with the turkey being carved at the head of the table.

SPICY CHICKEN FINGERS

Who needs to go out for chicken wings when you can make these? Use chicken breast meat instead and make them as hot as you wish—you've got a cool blue-cheese dressing to temper the heat.

2 cups **vegetable oil** 500 mL
4 **small boneless, skinless chicken breasts**
½ cup **all-purpose flour** 125 mL
salt & pepper
2 **large eggs**

1½ cups **panko (Japanese breadcrumbs) or cornflake crumbs** 375 mL
2 Tbsp **butter** 30 mL
1 clove **garlic, minced**
2–3 Tbsp **hot sauce** 30–45 mL
to serve **Blue Cheese Onion Dip (see facing page)**

Heat the oil in a deep, heavy-bottomed pot over medium-high heat (oil should be at least 2 inches (5 cm) deep but come up no higher than halfway) until temperature reads 365°F (185°C). Slice the chicken into fingers just under a ¾-inch (2 cm) thickness.

Put the flour in one bowl, whisk the eggs with 3 Tbsp (45 mL) water in another bowl, and put the breadcrumbs or cornflake crumbs in a third bowl. Season each bowl. Dip each finger in the flour, then the whisked egg, and then the crumbs, shaking off excess. Carefully place the chicken in batches of about 6 fingers at a time into the oil and cook, turning once, until cooked through, 3 to 4 minutes per side. Remove on a paper towel to drain.

(If you don't wish to deep-fry the fingers, you can pan-fry or oven-bake them. In a 375°F [190°C] oven, they take about 20 minutes. Turn once halfway through cooking.)

Melt the butter with garlic, and stir in hot sauce. While fingers are still hot, toss with the butter mixture to coat. Serve with Blue Cheese Onion Dip.

Serves 4

BLUE CHEESE ONION DIP

3 oz **blue cheese** 90 g
1 Tbsp **lemon juice** 15 mL
¼ cup **sour cream or yogurt** 60 mL
¼ cup **chopped green onion** 60 mL
2 tsp **chopped fresh oregano** 10 mL
salt & pepper

Pulse blue cheese, lemon juice and sour cream or yogurt in a food processor until smooth. Pulse in green onion and oregano and season to taste.
Makes about ½ cup (125 mL)

TASTE Living so close to the U.S. border, I've had my share of authentic Buffalo wings. I believe the secret to their tastiness lies in the tossing with melted butter along with the hot sauce—the sauce coats the outside of the wing without soaking in and ruining the crispiness. I've done the same with these fingers.

TECHNIQUE Most breaded foods follow this three-bowl technique: coating the item in flour creates a moisture barrier to allow the egg to stick, and the egg clearly works to fasten the final crumb coating. I've chosen panko or cornflake crumbs because either makes for a super-crunchy exterior.

TALE Michael and I have been known to haunt a few local places famous for their chicken wings. The Elbow Room in Welland, Ontario, has a style of wing that we have to make a special request for—it's not listed on the menu. Their "Bee's Wings" are supercrispy and dusted with Montreal steak spice. An order of these and an order of their really hot wings and we're in heaven (extra blue-cheese dressing, of course).

BEER & CHEDDAR STUFFED CHICKEN BREAST

Call this a "Canadian Chicken Kiev" (Chicken Winnipeg? Chicken Kenora?). The traditional chicken Kiev is a chicken breast stuffed with butter and herbs, but chicken that oozes melted cheese when you slice into it can't be beat.

2 cups **grated old white cheddar cheese** 500 mL
4 oz **cream cheese** 125 g
¼ cup **dark beer** 60 mL
1 Tbsp **grainy mustard** 15 mL
⅓ cup **finely chopped green onion** 80 mL
6 **chicken breasts, bone-in, skin-on**
1½ cups **loosely packed spinach leaves** 375 mL
salt & pepper

BEER CHEDDAR SAUCE

1¼ cups **dark beer** 310 mL
2 cups **grated old white cheddar cheese** 500 mL
2 Tbsp **cornstarch** 30 mL
2 tsp **grainy mustard** 10 mL
salt & pepper

Preheat the oven to 375°F (190°C). In a food processor, pulse the cheddar and cream cheese, and then add the beer and mustard to combine. Pulse in green onion. Remove the bone from each chicken and slice into the top to create a pocket. Line the inside of the chicken breast with a layer of spinach leaves to enclose. Place about ¼ cup (60 mL) of the cheese mixture over the leaves. Place chicken portions into a lightly greased baking dish skin side up and season lightly. Bake uncovered for 30 to 40 minutes, or until the chicken reaches an internal temperature of 180°F (82°C).

While the chicken is baking, prepare the sauce. In a saucepan, bring the beer slowly up to a simmer over medium heat. Toss the cheddar cheese with the cornstarch in a bowl and stir into the beer until melted. Stir in any pan juices from the baked chicken, the mustard, season to taste and serve, spooned over chicken. *Serves 6*

TASTE The combination of cream cheese, cheddar and beer makes for a very fonduelike filling, not to mention the beer and cheddar sauce.

TECHNIQUE The spinach doesn't just add color or a great flavor to the dish, it creates a nice little lining that helps to keep the cheese mixture inside the chicken. If a little does leak out, that's all right. You can stir it into the juices that cook out of the chicken, and you have more to add to the cheese sauce. Fabulous!

TALE Between the sauce and the chicken, this recipe calls for one full beer. A natural (and very Canadian) beverage pairing with this dish would be a cold, tall glass of the same.

TURKEY SALTIMBOCCA PINWHEELS

This entrée is relatively easy to make—it can be assembled ahead of time but presents well on the plate, which makes it ideal for your entertaining repertoire.

In a mortar and pestle, a small food processor or with the side of a chef's knife, crush the garlic with the sage leaves, a sprinkle of salt and pepper and 1 Tbsp (15 mL) olive oil, until it's a coarse paste.

Working with 1 at a time, spread out turkey cutlets onto a work surface with the short side nearest you, and spread the sage paste over each in a thin layer. Place a slice of prosciutto over each cutlet. Roll up the cutlets starting from the bottom and secure with a toothpick. Season the outside of the rolls.

Preheat the oven to 375°F (190°C). Heat an ovenproof sauté pan over medium-high heat and add 2 Tbsp (30 mL) olive oil. Place the turkey portions in the pan and sear, turning to brown all sides. Place the entire pan in the oven and roast, uncovered, until the turkey has cooked to a temperature of 180°F (82°C), 18 to 20 minutes.

Remove from the oven but keep the turkey portions in the pan. Add lemon juice and remaining 1 Tbsp (15 mL) olive oil. Stir to coat the turkey with the pan juices (there will just be a little), then remove from pan. Remove the toothpicks, and slice portions on the bias to serve.

Serves 4

4 cloves **garlic**
¼ cup **fresh sage leaves**
  60 mL
salt & pepper
4 Tbsp **olive oil, divided**
  60 mL
4 **turkey scallopini cutlets (see Technique on page 114), about 5 oz (150 g each)**
4 slices **prosciutto ham**
1 Tbsp **lemon juice** 15 mL

TASTE Unlike the original saltimbocca that uses whole sage leaves, I prefer to crush the sage into a paste with garlic and oil. I made this adjustment because I can sometimes find sage overpowering. And since the sage is spread around the entire surface of the scallopini, each bite has a proportionate, subtle taste of sage.

TECHNIQUE I've also taken liberties with the presentation of saltimbocca (I hope I can be forgiven). Typically saltimbocca is a cutlet topped with whole sage leaves and a slice of prosciutto baked on top, and the prosciutto ends up being a little chewy by the time it hits the table. By rolling the scallopini, the prosciutto is there but on the inside so it stays soft and tender.

TALE You can make saltimbocca with almost anything. While veal is traditional, it can be done with pork, chicken and even fish like halibut.

GARLIC ROASTED TURKEY CROWN WITH CHARDONNAY PAN SAUCE

The crown of turkey is merely the two turkey breasts left on the bone, but with the legs and thighs removed. Since most people favor white meat, this is a great choice if you are cooking for a crowd. Also, since breast meat cooks faster than dark meat, you don't have to worry about it drying out like you would if you were cooking a whole turkey.

1 head **fresh garlic, cloves peeled**	salt & pepper
¼ cup + 2 Tbsp **butter,** at room temperature 80 mL	1 **turkey crown,** about 6–8 lb (2.7–3.5 kg)
1 bunch **green onions,** trimmed, white and green parts separate	1 cup **Chardonnay** (preferably lightly oaked) 250 mL
2 Tbsp **chopped fresh tarragon** 30 mL	1 cup **chicken** (or turkey) **stock** (see page 3) 250 mL

Preheat the oven to 375°F (190°C).

In a food processor, pulse 4 cloves garlic with butter, green parts of green onions and tarragon to blend and season to taste. Reserve 2 Tbsp (30 mL) of this green-onion butter for the sauce. Place the white parts of green onions in an ungreased roasting pan and place the turkey crown on top. Insert the remaining garlic cloves into the cavity of the turkey crown. Using your fingers, gently create a pocket between the skin and the turkey breast and slather breast with garlic butter. Season the top of the crown and roast, covered with the lid or foil for 20 minutes. Remove the cover, reduce the oven temperature to 325°F (160°C) and cook, basting often, until turkey meat reaches an internal temperature of 175°F (80°C), about 90 minutes. Remove the turkey from the pan and place on a cutting board to rest while preparing sauce.

Remove green onions from the pan and discard. Remove excess fat from the pan juices using a spoon, and place the roasting pan with the skimmed pan juices on medium heat. Add the wine and reduce by half, stirring to pull up the caramelized bits from the bottom of the pan. Add the stock and bring up to a simmer. Remove the pan from the heat and stir in the reserved 2 Tbsp (30 mL) of green-onion butter. Serve spooned over sliced turkey. *Serves 6 to 8*

TASTE The Chardonnay adds typical wine flavor but is a little softer than a Riesling or other crisp white with high acidity. When I think Chardonnay, I think buttery with a hint of oak.

TECHNIQUE This roasted turkey is served with more of a restaurant-style *jus* or sauce, as opposed to a "gravy." If you love your gravy (and I do), whisk 1½ Tbsp (23 mL) cornstarch with a bit of the chicken stock. Add this along with the rest of the chicken stock to the sauce, making sure it comes up to a full boil and that you whisk constantly.

TALE My good friend Lisa avoids cooking turkey at holiday time, just because it's the "same old, same old." So I made this for her recently (and I didn't need a holiday as an excuse to make it, either), and she swears this will become her new staple when the in-laws come for Thanksgiving.

PHOTO Garlic Roasted Turkey Crown *served with* Moroccan Spiced Parsnips (page 148), Mascarpone Rough-Mashed Potatoes (page 125) *and* Plum Conserve (page 203)

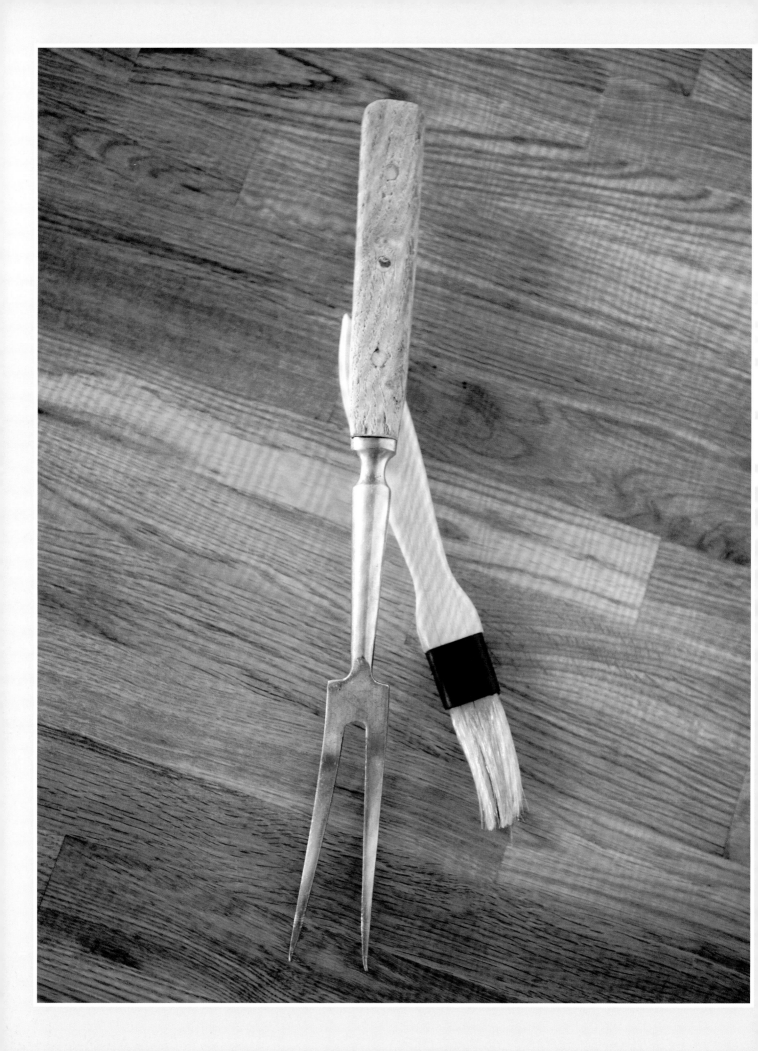

[MEAT]

I have a confession: we eat a lot of red meat in our house. We can't help it. Michael and I both love it.

And it helps to be pals with your butcher. Our local butcher, Hommer Van der Meer, is a regular judge at the Royal Winter Fair held every November in Toronto. This past year he judged beef cattle, and he liked the Blue Ribbon–winning Red Angus steer so much that he bought it. He called us up a few days afterwards and kindly offered to set aside some of it for us. Of course, we gratefully accepted.

A week later, Michael popped by Hommer's to pick up something for dinner, but he also came home with our "Royal" order. Our freezer is now completely full with beef. To make room, we had to toss old frozen corn and peas, rearrange fruit I had frozen and remove my ice cream freezer unit—and we have a big freezer.

I haven't had to buy beef for almost three months now. In case you're wondering why you haven't seen us for awhile, Hommer, we've got about two more months' inventory to get through.

ANNA'S POT ROAST

I like to serve this supper in a large soup plate so that it's easy to chase around the sauce with a bread roll (see page 155 for a recipe) or dumplings (page 123). Try horseradish as a perky accompaniment.

THE FIRST BRAISE

3½ lb **boneless blade or chuck beef roast, tied** 1.75 kg

salt & pepper

2 Tbsp **vegetable oil** 30 mL

1 **medium onion, roughly chopped**

1 rib **celery, roughly chopped**

2 **medium carrots, peeled and roughly chopped**

2 cloves **garlic, minced**

2 sprigs **fresh thyme**

2 **bay leaves**

1 cup (or more) **chicken or beef stock (low-sodium preferred)** 250 mL (or more)

1 can **(28 oz/796 mL) diced tomato**

VEGETABLES

1 lb **mini potatoes, cut into quarters** 500 g

2 **medium carrots, peeled and cut into ½-inch (1 cm) batons**

2 **medium parsnips, peeled and cut into ½-inch (1 cm) batons**

2 **medium white turnips, peeled and cut into wedges**

1 bottle **(12 oz/341 mL) dark beer**

TO SERVE

1 Tbsp **butter** 15 mL

salt & pepper

Fluffy Dumplings (see page 123, optional)

horseradish, as accompaniment

Preheat the oven to 325°F (160°C), and season all sides of the roast. Heat a heavy-bottomed pot (an ovenproof Dutch oven is preferred) over medium-high heat and add the oil, heating for 1 minute. Add the roast and sear for 2 minutes on each side until browned.

Remove the roast and reduce the heat to medium. Add the onion, celery and carrots, and stir until the onions are translucent, about 5 minutes. Add the garlic, thyme and bay leaves and stir 1 minute more. Return the roast to the pot and pour in the chicken or beef stock and diced tomato. Add more stock or water if necessary so that the liquid comes halfway up the roast. (It's fine if it's more than halfway, just so long as the roast is not completely

[continued next page . . .]

submerged). Cover the pot and bring liquid up to a simmer. Transfer the pot to the oven and cook for at least 3 hours, turning roast over after 1½ hours. (If you're not using an ovenproof pot, transfer the contents of the pot to a baking dish or roasting pan, and cover tightly with foil.)

After 2 hours of cooking, remove the roast from the pot. Strain the liquid to remove the first batch of vegetables—they will be mushy and will have already given out their full flavor and nutritive value. Return the liquid to the pot, skimming off excess fat. Stir in the potatoes, carrots, parsnips and turnips along with the dark beer, and return the roast to the pot. Cover and continue cooking in the oven until the roast and vegetables both yield easily when prodded with a fork, about 30 minutes.

To serve, transfer the roast to a cutting board and cover with foil. Remove the vegetables with a slotted spoon to a serving dish and toss with butter, then season and cover to keep warm. (If preparing dumplings, transfer the roast to a separate pan and put it in the oven, covered, along with the vegetables, with the heat turned off to keep warm while the dumplings cook in the braising liquid on top of the stove.) Untie the roast, slice and serve with the vegetables, sauce (the braising liquid) and horseradish on the side. *Serves 6*

TASTE Replacing the vegetables midway through cooking is important. After spending two hours simmering away, the first round of vegetables have given everything they can to the pot, and the taste and texture make them unpalatable. The new vegetables also add even more flavor to the pot, and they take in richer flavor as they cook to a perfect tenderness.

TECHNIQUE A blade roast is one of those tough cuts that benefit most from braising, and the longer you cook it, the better. When meat braises, much of the moisture starts to cook out into the liquid, giving great flavor but leaving a dry, tough roast. But keep that roast braising another hour and a half, and the moisture absorbs back into the meat, making it tender and juicy.

TALE I like making dumplings for chicken stew, but the first time I decided to make them in this pot roast, I was impressed. The flour from the dumplings works gently into the liquid, thickening it to a perfect consistency.

ASIAN GRILLED BEEF FLANK
STEAK The simple combination of garlic, ginger and fresh cilantro with just a touch of sesame oil turns this into a great grilling steak. I like to serve grilled flank steak alongside a hearty salad.

Stir the vinegar, soy sauce and mustard in a large baking or casserole dish. Peel and slice the onion, garlic and ginger and stir in. Tear in cilantro leaves and stir in. Whisk in the oil and chili flakes. Add the flank steak and spoon some of the marinade, including the garlic, ginger and onions overtop. Cover the dish and chill for at least 2 hours (and up to 12 hours) before grilling, turning steak once or twice.

To cook, preheat the barbecue to high. Grill the steak about 5 minutes on each side, not cooking past medium—see Taste). Let the steak rest on a cutting board for 3 minutes before slicing on the bias (i.e., against the grain).

Season well before serving. You may wish to serve the steak slices right on top of a salad. *Serves 6 to 8*

1 cup **rice wine vinegar** 250 mL
¼ cup **soy sauce** 60 mL
2 Tbsp **Dijon mustard** 30 mL
1 **medium onion**
6 cloves **garlic**
2-inch piece **fresh ginger** 5 cm piece
½ bunch **fresh cilantro**
2 Tbsp **sesame oil** 30 mL
red chili flakes
1 **beef flank steak, about 2 lb (1 kg)**
salt & pepper

TASTE Most tough cuts of beef should be braised, but flank steak can be grilled, and its flavor shines when grilled rare to medium-rare. (Anything over medium would make the steak too tough and too dry.) And the marinade just accentuates that rich beef flavor.

TECHNIQUE Generally the rule goes that the higher up on the trunk of the animal, the more tender the cut, and conversely, the lower on the animal, the tougher the cut. So it follows that tenderloin, strip loin and rib-eye are all tender, as they are located on the upper, less-exercised part of the animal and the flank, which is located at the belly, is tougher. The coarse grain and lack of fat of flank steak show that it is a well-exercised muscle, but with a little marinating and careful grilling you can have a tender steak. It also helps to slice the steak against the grain.

TALE This is a great steak to serve for a long weekend BBQ buffet. I like to slice it thinly and set it out on the table—that way everyone gets a taste and it's easier to eat than a whole steak for each guest.

NEW YORK STRIP LOIN WITH BÉARNAISE

Sometimes the best meals are the simplest: a good roasted chicken, fresh pasta with a quick, fresh tomato sauce, or a great cut of beef grilled just to your liking with a buttery sauce to go with it. Ah, perfection.

4 **center-cut New York strip loin steaks, about 10 oz (300 g) each, preferably 1 inch (2.5 cm) thick**
coarse salt and cracked black pepper
2 Tbsp **chopped fresh chives, for garnish** 30 mL

BÉARNAISE SAUCE
⅔ cup **butter** 160 mL
2 **large egg yolks**
3 Tbsp **lemon juice** 45 mL
2 Tbsp **white wine** 30 mL
1½ **Tbsp chopped fresh tarragon** 23 mL
salt & pepper

Pull the steaks from the refrigerator 30 minutes before grilling. Preheat the barbecue to high.

Prepare the Béarnaise sauce just before you cook the steaks. Melt the butter in the microwave (or melt gently on the stove without stirring), and cool for at least 5 minutes. Bring 2 inches (5 cm) of water up to a boil in a saucepan. In a metal or glass bowl that fits snugly on top of the saucepan, whisk the egg yolks, lemon juice and wine. Place the bowl over the boiling water (checking to see that the bottom of bowl is not touching the water), and whisk until the eggs are doubled in volume and hold a ribbon when the whisk is lifted from the bowl, about 2 minutes.

Remove the bowl from the heat and slowly add the melted butter in a thin stream while whisking, stopping to pour when only the milk solids or the white liquid portion of the melted butter is left. (If your sauce either becomes too thick or starts to "split," i.e., the butter starts separating from the sauce, pour 2 to 3 Tbsp [30 to 45 mL] of warm water into the center of the sauce bowl while gently whisking. Gradually use wider strokes to work it into the rest of the sauce. Add more water if needed.) Whisk in the tarragon and season to taste. Keep in a warm place (but not over direct heat) until ready to serve.

Season steaks on both sides and grill, about 6 minutes per side for medium-rare (depends on the temperature of the grill and the thickness of the steaks). After 3 minutes on one side, turn steaks 90 degrees to create nice grill marks. Steaks can be served whole or sliced for presentation. Sprinkle with chives. *Serves 4*

TASTE A Béarnaise is simply a hollandaise sauce with tarragon in it, and why it works so well with a grilled steak is an absolute mystery. I am simply content to just accept that it does.

TECHNIQUE A Béarnaise is a cooked emulsion of egg yolks with melted butter. The acidity of the wine and lemon juice prevent the yolk from overcooking, and you must add the butter gradually for it to incorporate. I find the best ratio is ⅓ cup (80 mL) butter for every yolk—any more and the sauce becomes heavy and greasy, and any less and it doesn't have enough body.

TALE Making this into a Steak Frites is the only way to improve on this simple meal. Try my frites recipe (page 126), which are delicious dunked in the Béarnaise, or else with a side of mayonnaise.

PHOTO New York Strip Loin
with Béarnaise *served with* Frites
(page 126)

BEEF STROGANOFF (WHEN'S THE LAST TIME YOU HAD IT?)

I think beef Stroganoff has been turned into too many instant and frozen entrées that we've forgotten how delicious it can be. And Stroganoff is actually easy to make—it only takes one pan (plus the pasta pot) and comes together as quickly as any prefab version.

2 Tbsp **olive oil** 30 mL
2 Tbsp **butter** 30 mL
1½ lb **beef sirloin, cut into ¼-inch (6 mm) strips** 750 g
2 Tbsp **all-purpose flour** 30 mL
1 cup **diced onion** 250 mL

3 cups **sliced cremini mushrooms** 750 mL
2 tsp **chopped fresh thyme** 10 mL
1 **bay leaf**
1½ cups **chicken or beef stock** 375 mL

⅔ cup **sour cream (14% M.F., not low fat)** 160 mL
salt & pepper
12 oz **wide egg noodles (dried)** 375 g
2 Tbsp **chopped fresh Italian parsley** 30 mL

Heat the oil and butter in a large sauté pan (with straight sides) over medium-high heat. Toss the beef with the flour and add to the pan, cooking until browned. Remove from the pan, reduce heat to medium and then add the onion, sautéing until browned. Add the mushrooms and sauté until tender, about 5 minutes. Add the reserved beef, along with the thyme, bay leaf and stock and bring up to a simmer, cooking uncovered for 10 minutes. Stir in sour cream and season to taste.

While the Stroganoff is simmering, boil the egg noodles in salted water until al dente. Drain and stir into the Stroganoff after the sour cream has been added. Garnish with chopped parsley before serving.

Serves 4

TASTE I love sour cream—it must be part of my heritage. Being of Eastern European descent, I think it's in my blood to want to put sour cream on just about everything.

TECHNIQUE Beef sirloin is one of those ideal, versatile cuts. It's not so delicate and tender that it can't be stewed or braised, but it's not so tough that you can't serve it as a steak. It also has great flavor, so if you're ever in doubt as to what cut to buy, you'll probably do just fine with sirloin.

TALE I made beef Stroganoff for the first time when my parents came to visit me in university one weekend. I splurged on the beef sirloin (to show my parents I wasn't *that* broke), and we sat in the little living room that I shared with six girls and ate over the coffee table. I'm certain the meal was more memorable for me than it was for my parents!

PORK TENDERLOIN WITH MAPLE ONION CREAM

When plated, this dish looks like it came out of a restaurant kitchen. The slices of pork tenderloin fanned out on the plate are gently blanketed with a subtle cream sauce. What a treat!

1 Tbsp **chopped fresh thyme** 15 mL

1 tsp **whole caraway seeds** 5 mL

½ tsp **fine salt, plus extra for seasoning** 2 mL

¼ tsp **ground white pepper, plus extra for seasoning** 1 mL

3 Tbsp **olive oil, divided** 45 mL

2 **pork tenderloins, about 1 lb (500 g) each**

1 Tbsp **butter** 15 mL

2 cups **sliced onion** 500 mL

¼ cup **white wine** 60 mL

3 Tbsp **maple syrup** 45 mL

1 cup **whipping cream (35%)** 250 mL

Preheat the oven to 375°F (190°C). In a small bowl stir the thyme, caraway seeds, salt, white pepper and 1 Tbsp (15 mL) olive oil to combine, and rub over the pork tenderloins. Place pork into an ungreased baking dish or roasting pan, and roast uncovered until it reaches an internal temperature of 165°F (74°C) (medium well), about 20 minutes. Remove pork from the baking dish to rest for 10 minutes before slicing.

While the pork is roasting, prepare the sauce. Heat the butter and the remaining 2 Tbsp (30 mL) of olive oil in a large sauté pan over medium heat. Add the onions and cook, stirring often, until lightly caramelized, about 20 minutes (see Taste). Add the wine and maple syrup and simmer until reduced by half—it will turn into a glaze. Add the cream and return to a simmer and season to taste.

To serve, slice the pork tenderloin into slices ½-inch (1 cm) thick and fan out onto 4 plates. Spoon the sauce over and serve. *Serves 4*

TASTE Typically I take much longer than 20 minutes (in fact, twice as long) to caramelize onions, but I find that the maple syrup adds a sweetness that is just right—if I were to cook the onions much longer, that sweetness would become too intense.

TECHNIQUE Dry rubs are a great way to add flavor to many cuts of meat at the last minute. The spices toast and cook into the meat, regardless of whether it is prepared in a pan, on the grill or in the oven.

TALE In cooking school I developed a great distaste for white pepper—it is called for in many sauces where you don't wish to see specks of black pepper. But I never minded that, and I always found ground white pepper tasted "dusty." It turns out it's probably because most ground white pepper sits on kitchen shelves so long that it goes stale. If you buy fresh, whole white peppercorns and use a pepper mill, you can truly appreciate (and now I can too) this superpeppery spice, which is even more intense than regular black pepper.

THE WORLD OF SCHNITZEL

A well-made schnitzel is a beautiful thing. It is fundamentally simple, but it's one of those meals I'll have a craving for, and I can't get the thought of it out of my head until I finally make it for myself.

Put the flour in one bowl, whisk the egg in another bowl and put the breadcrumbs or cornflake crumbs in a third bowl. Season each bowl.

Dip the cutlets in the flour, then the egg and then the breadcrumbs, shaking off excess. Heat 1½ Tbsp (23 mL) each oil and butter in a sauté pan over medium-high heat, until butter melts and then stops foaming. Add 2 breaded cutlets at a time and cook until golden brown on each side, turning after about 4 minutes. Season cooked cutlets lightly and serve with lemon on the side. *Serves 4*

1 cup **all-purpose flour** 250 mL

2 **large eggs**

1½ cups **dry breadcrumbs or cornflake crumbs** 375 mL

salt & pepper

4 **veal cutlets, about 6 oz (175 g) each, pounded thin (see Technique)**

3 Tbsp **vegetable oil** 45 mL

3 Tbsp **butter** 45 mL

1 **lemon, cut into quarters**

There are different versions of schnitzel, and the name of the dish changes depending on the additional sauce or topping. Here are the most common:

• **Jagerschnitzel**—*Jager* translates from German to mean "hunter," and anything made hunter-style implies the use of mushrooms. In this case, the schnitzel is slathered with a sauce of sautéed mushrooms and beef gravy.

• **Holsteinschnitzel**—Top the schnitzel with a fried egg, anchovy fillets, capers and lemon juice and you've got a hearty schnitzel, worthy of a sandwich. (bottom right)

• **Valdostanaschnitzel**—Just like chicken Cordon Bleu, except the ham and cheese are baked on top of the schnitzel. (bottom left)

• **Ziguenerschnitzel**—Topped with a tomato sauce laden with sliced onions and bell peppers, this "Gypsy-style" schnitzel would give even a good sausage on a bun a run for its money. (top right)

TASTE We were recently on a tropical cruise, where the food was exceptional. But I suddenly found myself craving the taste of schnitzel—who knows why. When we went to the dining room and were presented with that evening's menu, lo and behold there was a schnitzel course! It turns out that the executive chef was Austrian, and this menu was a tribute to home. (And the schnitzel was fabulous.)

TECHNIQUE If you can't buy your veal in scallopini form (i.e., thinly sliced or pounded), then you're going to have to do it yourself. I find it easiest to place the cutlet in a resealable bag (but left unsealed) and then pound gently with the flat bottom of a heavy pot. Don't pound with the pot at an angle though, as you'll tear the cutlet. If you have a meat tenderizer, use the flat, not the patterned, side and gently coax the cutlet to as thin as possible.

TALE On a culinary trip to Germany with other Canadian chefs, we stopped at a *Gasthaus*. Half of us ordered the steak with Béarnaise sauce, and the other half, myself included, ordered the schnitzel. I was so in my glory that I poured someone's Béarnaise all over my schnitzel and gobbled it up. The other chefs stared at first, then gave it a try—what a hit. So now I have my own schnitzel: Olsonschnitzel! (For a recipe for Béarnaise, see page 110.)

LAMB & EGGPLANT MOUSSAKA

Moussaka is kind of like "Greek lasagne," with sliced eggplant in place of sheets of pasta. I do find that the flavor of moussaka improves if made a day ahead and then reheated, making it perfect for a potluck.

BÉCHAMEL SAUCE
3½ cups **2% milk** 875 mL
¼ tsp **freshly grated nutmeg** 1 mL
6 Tbsp **butter** 90 mL
7 Tbsp **all-purpose flour** 105 mL
1 cup **grated Parmesan cheese** 250 mL
salt & pepper
4 **egg yolks**

MOUSSAKA
2 **large eggplants, sliced** ½ inch (1 cm) thick
3 Tbsp + 2 Tbsp **olive oil, divided** 45 mL + 30 mL
2 lb **Yukon Gold potatoes, peeled** 1 kg
1 lb **ground lamb** 500 g
1 lb **lean ground beef** 500 g
1 cup **diced onion** 250 mL
1 cup **finely diced red bell pepper** 250 mL

2 cloves **garlic, minced**
½ cup **red wine** 125 mL
1 can **(28 oz/796 mL) crushed tomatoes**
1 cup **chicken stock (see page 3)** 250 mL
1 Tbsp **chopped fresh oregano** 15 mL
salt & pepper
extra olive oil for brushing

For the béchamel, heat the milk with nutmeg in a saucepan over medium heat until just below a simmer. While the milk is heating, melt the butter in another saucepan, and add the flour. Stir with a wooden spoon over medium heat until a slightly nutty aroma is noticeable (it shouldn't change color, however), about 4 minutes. Slowly whisk in about ½ cup (125 mL) of the hot milk, continuing to whisk until smooth. Whisk in another cup (250 mL) of milk, whisking until smooth. Slowly whisk in the remaining milk, and stir constantly until the sauce just begins to bubble. Remove from the heat, stir in the Parmesan and season to taste. Cool to room temperature, and whisk in the egg yolks. Set aside or chill until ready to use.

For the moussaka, preheat the oven to broil. Arrange the eggplant slices on a broiler pan or baking sheet and lightly brush the eggplant with 3 Tbsp (45 mL) olive oil on both sides. Broil the eggplant on the top rack of the oven for 2 to 3 minutes on each side, or until softened and browned. Cool to room temperature.

Boil the potatoes in salted water. Drain, cool and slice into ½-inch (1 cm) pieces.

Set the oven temperature to 375°F (190°C). In a large sauté pan, heat the remaining 2 Tbsp (30 mL) oil over medium heat. Add the ground lamb and beef and sauté until cooked through, about 8 minutes. Remove the ground meat from the pan and drain all but 2 Tbsp (30 mL) of the fat. Add the onion and red pepper and sauté until onions are translucent. Add the garlic and sauté 1 minute more. Add the red wine and cook, stirring, until almost all of the wine has evaporated or been absorbed. Add the ground meat, crushed tomatoes, chicken stock and oregano and simmer until just about 1 cup (250 mL) of liquid is left, about 15 minutes. Season to taste.

Lightly brush a 9- x 13-inch (3.5 L) baking dish with olive oil. Arrange a layer of potato slices at the bottom of the dish and then cover with slices of eggplant. Spoon half of the meat sauce over the eggplant, and then repeat with a layer of potato and eggplant. Spoon over the remaining meat sauce and top with a final layer of potato and eggplant (if there's enough—don't worry if there's not). Bake uncovered for 40 minutes, or until bubbling, pressing down on the moussaka at least once during the baking time to draw the juices up.

Remove from the oven and spread the cooled béchamel sauce over the moussaka. Bake 15 minutes more, or until the sauce has souffléd slightly and browned on top.

Let the moussaka sit for 20 minutes before slicing to serve. *Serves 8*

TASTE It's the creamy béchamel sauce that makes a good moussaka. When you cut into your serving with the fork, the béchamel sinks into the other layers so that its creaminess envelops every bite.

TECHNIQUE For a slightly easier version, I sometimes mash the cooked potatoes in a bowl with the béchamel sauce. This saves a step in assembly and is still just as tasty.

TALE Apparently, you can make a pretty good soup out of almost anything. Searching through the fridge for something to turn into supper, all I could find was leftover moussaka, but not quite enough for two. Into a soup pot went the moussaka, a tin of tomatoes and a little water. I brought it to a simmer and puréed it quickly and voilà: Moussaka Soup! I've heard about the same being done to cabbage rolls, too.

ROASTED LEG OF LAMB WITH SPRING HERB STUFFING

Spring brings on my cravings for fresh, light herbs. Some of the first to peek out of the garden are chives, mint and tarragon, so it's natural to use them together.

one 2½ lb (1.1 kg) boneless lamb leg
½ cup **balsamic vinegar** 125 mL
1 **lemon, sliced**
salt & pepper

STUFFING
3 Tbsp **butter** 45 mL
2 cups **diced leeks, white and light green parts only (but reserve dark green parts)** 500 mL
½ cup **finely diced celery** 125 mL

1 tsp **finely grated lemon zest** 5 mL
2 tsp **finely grated fresh ginger** 10 mL
1 tsp **fine salt, plus extra for seasoning lamb** 5 mL
½ tsp **ground black pepper, plus extra for seasoning lamb** 2 mL
5 cups **finely diced egg bread (day-old)** 1.25 L
3 Tbsp **chopped fresh chives** 45 mL
3 Tbsp **chopped fresh mint** 45 mL

1 Tbsp **chopped fresh tarragon** 15 mL
1 Tbsp **chopped fresh marjoram (or oregano)** 15 mL
2 **large eggs**
1½ cups **chicken stock (see page 3)** 375 mL
1 cup **crumbled feta cheese** 250 mL
olive oil
juice of 1 lemon

Open up the lamb leg and place in a flat dish. Sprinkle with balsamic vinegar and place the lemon slices overtop. Cover and marinate in the refrigerator for 2 to 6 hours, turning occasionally.

For the stuffing, heat the butter in a medium sauté pan over medium heat. Add the leeks, celery and lemon zest and sweat until tender, about 5 minutes. Stir in the ginger, salt and pepper, and then toss these vegetables in a large bowl with the egg bread. Toss in the fresh herbs. In a small bowl, whisk the eggs to blend and then add to the bread mixture along with the chicken stock. Stir in the feta.

To stuff, remove the lamb from the marinade, pat dry and season lightly. Press together the stuffing in your hands and place along the center of the lamb. Roll up the lamb and tie with butcher's twine to secure.

To roast, preheat the oven to 350°F (180°C). Arrange the reserved dark green leek parts at the bottom of a roasting pan, and place the tied lamb leg on top. Brush the lamb with olive oil and sprinkle generously with salt and pepper. Roast until stuffing reaches an internal temperature of 130°F (54°C) (or about 145°F [63°C] for medium). Squeeze lemon juice over the lamb and let rest for 15 minutes before removing the twine and slicing. *Serves 8 to 10*

TASTE Egg bread makes great stuffing—it has great color, is tender and rich and complements those springtime herbs perfectly.

TECHNIQUE Boneless lamb leg usually comes tied; simply cut away the ties to open up the lamb for the marinating and stuffing. When re-tying, your handiwork doesn't have to be as adept as a butcher's—just be sure it's secure.

TALE Both Michael and I grew up not eating a lot of lamb, though we certainly enjoy it now. I think the generation before us had to suffer through more *mutton* than lamb, which is a stronger and tougher meat.

PHOTO Roasted Leg of Lamb *served with* Cucumber with Sour Cream, Lime & Basil (page 31)

[STARCHES & SIDES]

Too often we plan our meal around the main protein, giving it lots of attention and letting it determine the entire flavor scheme. Possibly we do this since it requires the largest financial commitment, and therefore we feel it is owed more focus.

But we still can invest some time and effort in preparing potatoes, pasta and rice. In fact, we sometimes need to give our side dishes a little more attention to make our meals more interesting.

I *love* side dishes, actually. Before I delved into the world of pastry, my time spent in the professional kitchen was often as "Chef Entremetier"—in charge of preparing starches and side dishes. I would revel in creating accompanying foods to match with each evening's featured proteins. The choices were endless. I would walk around the giant walk-in cooler and haunt the dry goods pantry, searching for new ingredients to bring together or ordinary ingredients to apply new techniques to.

FLUFFY DUMPLINGS

These are ideal sauce sponges, traditionally a part of chicken stew. You can also try the dumplings with pot roast (page 107). Both the stew and the roast are great braising dishes to have in winter.

1 cup **all-purpose flour** 250 mL	2 Tbsp **olive oil or vegetable oil** 30 mL
2 tsp **baking powder** 10 mL	3 Tbsp **finely chopped green onion or fresh parsley** 45 mL
½ tsp **fine salt** 2 mL	
⅔ cup **2% milk** 160 mL	

Sift the dry ingredients into a bowl. Add the milk, oil and green onion (or parsley) and stir just until blended. The dough will be very sticky. When your stew is nearly done, drop spoonfuls of dumpling dough over the braising liquid that is simmering. (If you are making these with the pot roast [page 107], do this step after the roast and vegetables have been removed from the pot.) Cover the pot and simmer for 10 to 12 minutes. Do not lift the lid until at least the first half of cooking time is over—see Technique. *Makes about 6 dumplings*

TASTE Dumplings don't have to be plain. For a kick, add 1 tsp (5 mL) of chopped fresh rosemary, sage or dill.

TECHNIQUE This style of dumpling dough should be wet and sticky, not dense like biscuit or bread dough. And though you might be tempted to lift the lid off the pot to check on your dumplings, wait at least 6 minutes before taking a peek so that none of the steam escapes from the pot.

TALE It's taken me a while to become adept at making dumplings. I certainly know about stodgy dumplings from experience. Too often I would judge the dumpling mix too wet, thinking they would cook up soggy and squishy, so I would always add a bunch of flour. But they would end up being dry little "pellets" (sounds yummy, huh?). Trust me, the wetter, the better.

LOADED POTATO BAKE

Love an overstuffed, loaded baked potato? Also love creamy, scalloped potatoes? This melds the best of both worlds.

Preheat the oven to 350°F (180°C) and grease a 11- x 7-inch (2 L) baking dish.

In a medium, heavy-bottomed saucepan over medium heat, cook the bacon until crisp. Remove from the pan and reserve. Increase the heat to medium-high and sauté the onion in the bacon drippings until tender and lightly browned, about 5 minutes. Add garlic and cook 1 minute more. Add the milk and bring up to a simmer. Remove from the heat, whisk in the sour cream and season lightly.

To assemble, spoon a little of the milk mixture in the bottom of the prepared baking dish and arrange a single layer of sliced potatoes on top. Spoon another layer of milk mixture over the potatoes and sprinkle with a bit of reserved bacon, green onion and cheddar cheese. Top with another layer of potatoes and continue layering with the milk mixture, bacon, green onion, cheddar and potatoes, finishing with a final sprinkling of cheddar. Place a piece of parchment directly on top of the cheese and then cover dish with foil (or lid). Bake for 45 minutes, then remove the foil and parchment and bake for another 20 to 30 minutes, or until a knife inserted in the center of the dish yields easily. Let cool for 15 minutes before serving. *Serves 8 to 10*

6 slices **bacon, diced**
1 cup **diced onion** 250 mL
2 cloves **garlic, minced**
2 cups **2% milk** 500 mL
1½ cups **sour cream (14% M.F., not low fat)** 375 mL
salt & pepper
3 lb **Yukon Gold potatoes, peeled and sliced as thinly as possible** 1.5 kg
1 cup **chopped green onion** 250 mL
2 cups **grated medium cheddar cheese** 500 mL

TASTE While cheddar cheese may be a more traditional baked potato topper, I also like to use Swiss or even a little blue cheese in its place.

TECHNIQUE Yukon Gold potatoes are usually my top pick for a dish such as this, not just for the taste but because they have just the right amount of starch to hold together when they cook.

TALE When I go out to a restaurant that offers "your choice of baked potato, mashed potato, fries or rice," I *always* choose baked potato, and always "fully loaded." It's that classic combination of sour cream, bacon, green onion and cheese that makes a humble potato special.

MASCARPONE ROUGH-MASHED POTATOES
These mashed potatoes aren't the smooth, whipped style. They're coarse, lumpy and absolutely delicious.

1½ lb **red mini potatoes, peel on** 750 g
1 clove **garlic, sliced**
3 Tbsp **butter, in pieces** 45 mL

¾ cup **mascarpone cheese** 190 mL
1 **green onion, chopped**
salt & pepper

Cut mini potatoes in quarters, and add potatoes along with the garlic to a pot with salted water. Bring to a boil and then simmer until potatoes are tender, about 10 minutes. Drain and return the potatoes and garlic to the pot. Add the butter and, using a fork, roughly mash the potatoes and melt in the butter. Stir in the mascarpone and green onion, again roughly mashing—lumps should be visible. Season to taste and serve. *Serves 4*

TASTE The sweetness and richness of mascarpone cheese makes these potatoes truly deca-dent. If you think they might be too rich for your invited crowd, substitute with yogurt for a lower-fat, tangier version. (However, make sure you use a whole-milk yogurt.)

TECHNIQUE Here it's all about *roughly* mashing the potatoes. Mini potatoes turn "gluey" if mashed in the traditional fashion, so by stirring the minis with a fork, you won't wreak havoc with the texture. If you'd prefer smooth-mashed potatoes, use an equivalent measure of Yukon Gold potatoes, and feel free to use a potato masher or ricer.

TALE I find these a tasty, if unexpected, companion to fish. It doesn't always have to be rice.

FRITES

Maybe it's the chef in me, but I see making french fries at home as definitely worth the effort, especially if you are going to serve them alongside the New York Strip Loin with Béarnaise Sauce (page 110).

Cut the potatoes into ½-inch-wide (1 cm) batons and pat dry with paper towels. For the first "blanch," heat the oil to 350°F (180°C) in a deep, heavy-bottomed pot, large enough that the oil only comes up halfway. Add half the potatoes and deep-fry just until the potatoes are cooked through and tender, about 5 minutes—the fries will not brown at this point. Remove the fries with a slotted spoon onto a paper towel–lined tray and repeat with the other half. Fries at this point can be chilled until ready for the second deep-fry.

Heat the oil to 375°F (190°C). Add half the fries and cook until golden brown, about 5 minutes. Remove from the oil with a slotted spoon, let drain on paper towels for a moment, then toss in a bowl with salt and pepper. Repeat with the remaining fries and serve immediately.

Serves 4 to 6

3 lb **Yukon Gold potatoes, peeled or unpeeled** 1.5 kg
6 cups **vegetable oil (see Taste)** 1.5 L
salt & pepper

TASTE Yes, it's a very simple list of ingredients! Let's talk about the oil. I admit I like deep-frying in peanut oil, although most restaurants have steered clear of it due to allergy concerns, and also price—it is far more expensive than other oils. However, at home I find myself most often using canola oil—it's clean-tasting and takes to high temperatures very well.

TECHNIQUE The first blanch is the key to a perfect fry. If you were to deep-fry potatoes in just one go, they would take a long time to cook, turning dark brown on the outside and never really becoming crispy. For a golden brown, crispy-on-the-outside, tender-on-the-inside french fry, a first blanch at a moderate heat is vital because it first cooks the potato through.

TALE I learned a great trick for deliciously dressed fries—while warm, toss them with a little Caesar salad dressing. Ooh, so scrumptious, but you have to gobble them up right away before they get too soggy.

CITRUS CORIANDER RICE Simple and fragrant, this beats your everyday white rice.

1 Tbsp **ground coriander**
15 mL

1 stem **lemongrass, bruised
(see Taste)**

1 Tbsp **fine salt** 15 mL

1½ cups **basmati white rice**
375 mL

2 Tbsp **olive oil** 30 mL

1 Tbsp **finely grated lemon
zest** 15 mL

¼ cup **lemon juice** 60 mL

¼ cup **chopped fresh
cilantro** 60 mL

pinch **red chili flakes
(optional)**

salt & pepper

Bring 6 cups (1.5 L) water, ground coriander, lemongrass and salt up to a boil in a saucepan. Rinse the rice in a fine strainer until the water runs clear and add to the boiling water. Once it returns to the boil, lower the heat and simmer the rice (uncovered is okay) for 10 minutes. Drain and rinse the rice through a fine strainer, discard the lemongrass and return to the pot over low heat. Stir in the olive oil, lemon zest and lemon juice. Stir in the chopped fresh cilantro and red chili flakes (if using) and season to taste. Serve warm or at room temperature. *Makes about 4 cups (1 L) of rice*

TASTE Lemongrass imparts a lovely fragrant lemony perfume to the rice as it cooks, but it never becomes tender no matter how long you cook it. Bruise the lemongrass by smashing it with the side of your knife—this extracts the flavors, and keeping it whole makes it easy to pull out of the rice before serving.

TECHNIQUE I confess—I am horrid at cooking regular rice. It has taken me this long to pick up on this particular and relatively foolproof way of cooking basmati rice, boiling it almost like pasta. It doesn't work with all rice varieties, however. I'll work on that and get back to you.

TALE I tailor this rice to a more Asian-inspired meal by stirring in ½ cup (125 mL) unsweetened coconut at the very end with the cilantro.

BACON & TOMATO GNOCCHI

This is simple, comfort food. Making potato gnocchi is much easier than making pasta, so try your hand at this if you've never made homemade pasta before. (The technique is different, but it's good practice.)

GNOCCHI

1 lb **russet potatoes (about 1 large, or 2 small)** 500 g
½ cup + 2 Tbsp **all-purpose flour** 125 mL + 30 mL
1 **large egg**
1½ tsp **extra virgin olive oil** 7.5 mL
½ tsp **finely grated lemon zest** 2 mL
½ tsp **fine salt** 2 mL
¼ tsp **ground black pepper** 1 mL
pinch **ground nutmeg**

SAUCE

3 slices **thick-cut bacon, diced**
2 cloves **garlic, minced**
½ cup **red wine** 125 mL
1 can **(28 oz/796 mL) diced tomato**
2 **bay leaves**
salt & pepper
½ cup **shaved Parmesan cheese** 125 mL

For the gnocchi, preheat the oven to 400°F (200°C). Pierce the potato in several places with a fork. Bake until tender, about 1 hour. Let stand until just cool enough to handle, about 15 minutes. Peel the potato, put in a medium bowl and mash with a fork until smooth (do not use a food processor). Add the flour, egg, olive oil, lemon zest, salt, pepper and nutmeg and stir just until blended. Turn out the dough on a lightly floured surface, and divide into 8 pieces. Take 1 piece and roll it between your hands and also on the work surface to a 12-inch (30 cm) long rope. Cut into ½-inch (1 cm) pieces. Place gnocchi on lightly floured baking sheet. Repeat with remaining dough. Gnocchi can be made up to 8 hours ahead and chilled. (You can also freeze the gnocchi at this point.)

For the sauce, sauté the bacon in a pan over medium-high heat until crisp. Remove the bacon and reserve. Reduce the heat to medium, add the garlic to the bacon drippings and stir for a moment. Add the wine carefully (it will sputter), and then the tomatoes and bay leaves. Simmer for 10 minutes, uncovered. Season to taste.

To cook the gnocchi, bring a pot of salted water to a boil. Add the gnocchi and cook until they float. Drain the gnocchi and add to sauce.

To serve, return the sauce to a simmer, add reserved bacon and garnish with Parmesan. *Serves 6 as an appetizer, 4 as an entrée*

TASTE I have no problem using canned tomatoes. Tomatoes for processing are harvested at their peak ripeness, so in winter especially, it's the best way to get a good tomato sauce. Try several brands to see which one you like best.

TECHNIQUE Russet potatoes are best for this because of their mealy texture. This may not sound appetizing, but that texture makes for a more tender gnocchi. After you've added the gnocchi to the sauce, try popping it in a 375°F (190°C) oven for 10 minutes. The gnocchi will soufflé beautifully.

TALE The combination of bacon and tomato is reminiscent of one of my favorite dishes I would regularly make when I was just learning to cook. It was a simple pasta dish with tomato sauce, bacon and fresh oregano (I had just discovered how tasty fresh herbs were), and I thought I had created something never before seen. It's a personal classic.

THREE-ONION COUSCOUS This couscous
makes a great companion to almost anything, whether grilled
meat or fish, fragrant stews or just fresh sliced vegetables, but it's
particularly wonderful with the Vegetable Tagine (see page 139),
which has a lot of spice, of chili heat, to it.

1 cup **dry couscous** 250 mL

2 tsp **lemon zest** 10 mL

2 Tbsp **olive oil, divided**
  30 mL

1 cup **chopped leeks, white
and light green parts only**
250 mL

½ cup **diced Vidalia onion**
  125 mL

4 Tbsp **chopped fresh
chives** 60 mL

salt & pepper

Pour 1 cup (250 mL) of boiling water over couscous in a medium bowl, stir in
the lemon zest, cover and let sit 10 minutes. Fluff with a fork and set aside.
Heat 1 Tbsp (15 mL) oil in a sauté pan over medium heat and sauté leeks
until tender, about 5 minutes. Remove from the pan and set aside. Add the
remaining 1 Tbsp (15 mL) oil to the pan and sauté Vidalia onion until lightly
caramelized, about 15 minutes. Add the onion to the couscous along with
the reserved leeks and fresh chives and stir. Season and chill until ready
to serve.

Couscous can be served cold or at room temperature, or warmed over
low heat in a sauté pan for 5 minutes. *Serves 6*

TASTE Each of the three alliums in this dish offers its own distinct characteristic to the
couscous. The leeks add a bright, mildly garlic note, the Vidalia a richer sweetness, and the
chives a delicate herbaceous quality.

TECHNIQUE Couscous is basically cooked durum semolina that is then rolled in flour.
The most commonly available couscous is quick-cooking, and only needs a quick soak in hot
water. Traditional couscous requires a lengthier steaming process.

TALE I regard couscous as convenience food. It takes no time to prepare and can be an
appropriate accompaniment to so many entrées.

PAPPARDELLE PASTA WITH SQUASH, RICOTTA & SAGE
The pancetta or bacon can be eliminated from this recipe to turn this into a vegetarian dish. I sometimes like to serve half portions of this recipe as an appetizer course.

¼ cup **diced pancetta (thickly sliced) or bacon** 60 mL

¼ cup **diced onion or shallot** 60 mL

1½ cups **diced butternut squash (¾ inch/2 cm dice)** 375 mL

1 clove **garlic, minced**

2 tsp **finely chopped fresh sage** 10 mL

¼ cup **white wine** 60 mL

12 oz **pappardelle pasta, or fresh lasagne sheets cut into 1-inch (2.5 cm) strips** 375 g

butter for tossing with pasta, plus 2 Tbsp (30 mL) **cold butter for sauce**

salt & pepper

⅔ cup **ricotta cheese** 160 mL

In a large sauté pan over medium-high heat, sauté pancetta or bacon until crispy, then remove from the pan and reserve. In the same pan, sauté the onion or shallot for 4 minutes to soften (do not let it brown), then add the diced squash. Add the garlic, fresh sage, wine and ½ cup (125 mL) water and cook for about 6 minutes, or until the squash is tender.

Meanwhile, cook pappardelle pasta or lasagne in boiling salted water until just tender. Drain, toss in a touch of butter, season and keep warm in a serving dish.

To finish the pasta sauce, reduce the heat to medium-low and stir in ricotta and the 2 Tbsp (30 mL) of cold butter. Season to taste and toss with pasta. Serve. *Serves 4*

TASTE The combination of squash and sage is a natural partner to a lightly oaked Chardonnay, but can pair equally well with Pinot Noir.

TECHNIQUE Pappardelle is the pasta I choose when I have a sauce with "bits and pieces"—I want to be able to wrap the sauce with the pasta for each bite. A delicate sauce suits a finer pasta, whereas the wide noodles of pappardelle suit the heartier squash and bacon.

TALE Having worked at an Italian restaurant, I was taught to remember my pasta widths a long time ago: pappardelle is twice the width of tagliatelle, tagliatelle is twice the width of fettucine and fettucine is twice the width of linguini.

LEMON MELON SEED PASTA WITH ASPARAGUS & CHÈVRE

This pasta is cooked in the style of risotto, that is, the liquid is added slowly. This allows you great control in taste and texture. Add some peeled shrimp (1 lb/450 g) with the asparagus to turn this into an entrée.

2 Tbsp **olive oil** 30 mL
1 cup **finely diced onion** 250 mL
½ cup **finely diced celery** 125 mL
1⅓ cups **dried "melon seed pasta"** (*semi di melone*) or other small pasta such as *acini di pepe* ("peppercorn") or orzo 330 mL
1 cup **white wine** 250 mL
2 tsp **finely grated lemon zest** 10 mL

2½ cups **chicken stock (see page 3) or vegetable stock** 625 mL
1 lb **fresh asparagus, cut into 1-inch (2.5 cm) pieces** 500 g
2 Tbsp **chopped fresh mint** 30 mL
2 Tbsp **chopped fresh chives** 30 mL
salt & pepper
juice of ½ lemon
2 Tbsp **butter** 30 mL
3 oz **chèvre** 90 g

Heat the olive oil in a large heavy-bottomed sauté pan over medium heat and add the onion and celery. Sauté until translucent, about 5 minutes. Add the uncooked pasta and stir to coat with the oil, about 2 minutes. Add the white wine and lemon zest and cook, stirring with a wooden spoon, until liquid has evaporated. Add the stock, 1 cup (250 mL) at a time, stirring until liquid absorbs after each addition. Add the asparagus with the last addition of stock. When the pasta is al dente (after about 10 minutes), stir in the mint and chives and season to taste. Stir in the lemon juice and butter. Spoon pasta into bowls and crumble chèvre on top. *Serves 4 as an appetizer or side dish*

TASTE This dish is a true taste of spring. I usually make this when it is full-on asparagus season and I am trying to find new ways to use it up.

TECHNIQUE Cooking pasta using the same method as with risotto may seem unusual but it works very well. The principle is exactly the same. The pasta is first sautéed to seal in the starch, the "first flood" of wine deglazes the pan and the gradual addition of stock slowly releases the starch in the pasta as it cooks, thickening the sauce a little and enabling you to control the cooking time so it doesn't lose its al dente finish.

TALE I picked up this technique from my husband Michael. On one of our first dates, he made me acini di pepe pasta with finely diced eggplant and tomato as an appetizer. Clearly it was delicious—worth marrying him for!

TOMATO BRUSCHETTA QUINOA The
simple flavors of a basic but delicious bruschetta—tomato, garlic, olive oil and herbs—can be translated to so many foods. Quinoa is a fabulous sponge for such a tasty combination.

1 cup **quinoa** 250 mL
3 cups **finely diced ripe tomato** 750 mL
3 **green onions, chopped**
1 clove **garlic, minced**
2 Tbsp **chopped fresh basil** 30 mL

2 Tbsp **chopped fresh cilantro** 30 mL
2 Tbsp **red wine vinegar** 30 mL
2 Tbsp **extra virgin olive oil** 30 mL
salt & pepper

Bring 4 cups (1 L) of salted water up to a boil. Rinse the quinoa and add to the water. Boil until tender, about 10 minutes, then strain and rinse to cool. Set aside.

Stir the remaining ingredients together in a bowl and season lightly. Add the quinoa, adjust seasoning and chill until ready to serve. *Serves 6*

TASTE Quinoa is known as an "ancient grain" (it was grown by the Incas), but it isn't actually a grain—rather, it's the seed of a plant. I find some grocery stores carry it, but it is most easily sourced at health food stores because it is high in protein as well as gluten free.

TECHNIQUE Minus the quinoa from this recipe and you have a great topping for bruschetta. To intensify the flavors, mix up the tomatoes with the other ingredients and let it sit refrigerated for an hour or two. Strain off the liquid into a small pan and reduce it down to a tablespoon or two. Add this to the tomato mixture and you've got bigger flavor.

TALE When I have a buffet-style dinner party in the summertime, I like to set out a range of salads. A salad such as this is visually appealing and is something a little bit different from the expected potato and pasta salads.

CRACKED WHEAT WITH ROASTED GARLIC, CHARRED CORN & BASIL

Cracked wheat isn't just for breakfast cereal. It's a great sponge for other flavors, and also makes a fabulous summer salad.

Bring 2 cups (500 mL) water up to a boil. Salt lightly and stir in the cracked wheat. Return to a boil and then simmer uncovered for 5 minutes. Remove from the heat, rinse to cool, then fluff with a fork.

Preheat a barbecue to medium heat. Toss the garlic cloves with 1 Tbsp (15 mL) olive oil and wrap in foil. Roast the garlic on the grill until browned and soft, about 20 minutes. While the garlic is roasting, grill the corn until cooked and grill marks are visible, about 5 minutes. Scrape corn kernels off the cobs and mix into a bowl with the cooled cracked wheat. Mash the roasted garlic with the remaining 1 Tbsp (15 mL) olive oil and stir into cracked wheat. Add the red pepper, tear in basil leaves (or cut it into a chiffonade—see Technique) and season to taste.

Serve chilled or at room temperature. *Serves 6*

1 cup **cracked bulgur wheat** 250 mL
3 cloves **garlic, peeled**
2 Tbsp **olive oil, divided** 30 mL
2 ears **fresh corn, husks removed**
½ cup **finely diced red bell pepper** 125 mL
1 cup **loosely packed fresh basil leaves** 250 mL
salt & pepper

TASTE This is one of those salads that improves as it sits. You can make it a day ahead, and the basil should remain bright green as the salad has no acidic ingredients to discolor it.

TECHNIQUE Another trick to help keep your basil green is to cut it in a *chiffonade*. Stack basil leaves on top of each other, roll them up lengthwise and then slice across the stem with a very sharp knife. This does less damage to the cells of the leaf than roughly chopping them, and the basil will stay green longer. This also works for mint and sage.

TALE The first time I prepared cracked wheat, I neglected to read any instructions and assumed it was the same as couscous. I soaked the cracked wheat in hot water, fluffed it up a bit with a fork and added my other ingredients. It was like chewing on raw oats. I've since learned not to make such assumptions.

PHOTO Top to bottom: Cracked Wheat with Roasted Garlic, Charred Corn & Basil (this page), Three-Onion Couscous (page 130), Tomato Bruschetta Quinoa (page 133)

[VEGETABLES]

Like a good vegetable medley, I have a little bit of everything in this chapter. Many of my vegetable concoctions are not just sides, but can also double as entrées, such as the Vegetable Tagine (page 139) and Spinach, Corn & Herbed Stuffed Peppers (page 143).

Good vegetables are all about seasonality. An asparagus dish prepared in May is far tastier because it is made with (hopefully) local, in-season asparagus. And a tomato salsa made with tomatoes in August that, if bought at the farmers' market, hold the heat of the sun, will overshadow any salsa made with underripe and/or imported tomatoes in January.

So pick your vegetable courses according to the time of year, or use my menu guide at the back of this book to steer you right. And borrow my mantra as often as you wish: *what grows together goes together*.

VEGETABLE TAGINE
This Moroccan stew is fragrant and rich tasting without being heavy. Serve it with the Three-Onion Couscous (page 130).

3 Tbsp **olive oil** 30 mL
2 cups **peeled and diced sweet potato (1-inch/ 2.5 cm dice)** 500 mL
1½ cups **chopped onion (1-inch/2.5 cm pieces)** 375 mL
1½ cups **chopped carrots (1-inch/2.5 cm pieces)** 375 mL
3 cloves **garlic, minced**
2 Tbsp **finely grated fresh ginger** 30 mL
1 Tbsp **ground cumin** 15 mL
1 Tbsp **ground coriander** 15 mL
¾ tsp **ground cinnamon** 4 mL

3 cups **vegetable stock or water** 750 mL
3 Tbsp **fancy molasses** 45 mL
1½ cups **cauliflower florets** 375 mL
1½ cups **diced eggplant (1-inch/2.5 cm dice)** 375 mL
1 can **(14 oz/398 mL) chickpeas, drained and rinsed**
¾ cup **raisins** 190 mL
½ cup **chopped dried apricots** 125 mL
salt & pepper
½ cup **sliced almonds, lightly toasted** 125 mL

Heat the oil in a large pot over medium heat. Add sweet potato, onion and carrots and sauté until onions are translucent, about 5 minutes. Add garlic, ginger, and ground spices and sauté 2 minutes. Add stock (or water) and molasses and bring up to a simmer. Add cauliflower, eggplant, chickpeas, raisins and apricots, season lightly, and bring up to a simmer. Lower the heat and continue simmering, covered, until all the vegetables are tender and most of the liquid has absorbed (but the tagine is still moist), about 20 minutes. Adjust the seasoning to taste and serve garnished with toasted almonds. *Serves 8 as a side dish, 4 as an entrée*

TASTE The raisins and apricots add a subtle sweetness to the tagine as does the cinnamon, but the spice is appropriately muted by the cumin, coriander, ginger and garlic.

TECHNIQUE *Tagine* actually refers to the cone-shaped dish that this stew is traditionally cooked in. The principle of it is simple—the steam from the stew rises up, condenses at the top of the cone-shaped lid and then slowly drips down the cone to return to the stew, so no moisture or flavor is lost.

TALE Adding diced chicken or diced, seared leg of lamb turns this dish into a delectable entrée.

CURRIED CAULIFLOWER WITH RAITA

This is a hearty cauliflower dish that warms you up on a cold day. The cucumber raita will cool you down if it's a little too spicy.

2 Tbsp **vegetable oil** 30 mL
2 Tbsp **garam masala (see Taste)** 30 mL
1 tsp **ground turmeric** 5 mL
1 Tbsp **finely grated fresh ginger** 15 mL
2 cloves **garlic, minced**
2 Tbsp **tomato paste** 30 mL
2 cups **yogurt** 500 mL

1 head **cauliflower, cut into florets**
1 **fresh chili pepper, seeded and finely chopped**
salt
2 Tbsp **chopped green onion, to garnish** 30 mL
2 Tbsp **chopped fresh cilantro, to garnish** 30 mL

RAITA
1½ cups **grated cucumber** 375 mL
1 cup **yogurt** 250 mL
2 Tbsp **chopped fresh mint** 30 mL
1 Tbsp **honey** 15 mL
salt & pepper

Heat the oil in a sauté pan over high heat. Add the garam masala, turmeric, ginger and garlic and stir for 15 seconds. Quickly stir in the tomato paste and then the yogurt. When the mixture begins to simmer, stir in the cauliflower and chili pepper and season lightly with salt. Cover and reduce the heat to medium, simmering until cauliflower is tender, about 15 minutes.

While the cauliflower in simmering, prepare the raita. Stir all the ingredients together in a bowl and season to taste.

Serve the cauliflower warm, garnished with green onion and fresh cilantro, with the raita on the side. *Serves 4 to 6*

TASTE Garam masala is simply a blend of spices, not a single spice (unlike allspice, which is actually a single spice). Store-bought garam masala typically has a familiar curry taste, but there are thousands of blends, often family recipes, passed down through generations.

TECHNIQUE If you want to make the raita a few hours ahead, grate the cucumber, salt it lightly and let it sit in a strainer over a bowl in the fridge for an hour or two. Then give it a good squeeze before stirring it into the other ingredients.

TALE I take advantage of the "flatness" of cauliflower so that other ingredients can shine. I have to admit, it's not one of my favorite vegetables—it's not that I don't like the taste or texture, I just find it rather bland on its own. (I believe it's not just me—I imagine that's why cheese sauce is the most popular accompaniment.) I think the richness of curry really brings out the best in cauliflower.

LEMON PESTO GRILLED SUMMER VEGETABLES

Using sunflower seeds instead of the traditional pine nuts is a nice twist on pesto. It works perfectly with the virtually full-color spectrum of summer vegetables available simultaneously in summertime.

LEMON PESTO

2 cups **loosely packed fresh basil leaves** 500 mL

1 cup **loosely packed fresh Italian parsley leaves** 250 mL

¼ cup **loosely packed fresh oregano** 60 mL

½ cup **chopped green onion** 125 mL

5 Tbsp **extra virgin olive oil** 75 mL

2 Tbsp **finely grated lemon zest** 30 mL

2 cloves **garlic, minced**

½ cup **unsalted sunflower seeds** 125 mL

salt & pepper

GRILLED VEGETABLES

1 **green zucchini**

1 **yellow zucchini**

1 **Japanese eggplant**

1 **red bell pepper**

1 **green bell pepper**

salt & pepper

For the lemon pesto, pulse the basil, parsley, oregano and green onion with olive oil in a food processor until blended. Add the lemon zest, garlic and sunflower seeds and pulse until it's a paste. Season to taste and chill until ready to use.

For the vegetables, preheat a barbecue on high. (Don't worry about brushing the vegetables with oil before grilling—see Technique). Slice the zucchini and eggplant ¼ inch (6 mm) thick on the bias, and seed the bell peppers and cut into 2-inch (5 cm) wedges. Grill the vegetables about 5 minutes on each side, or until grill marks are visible—it's all right if the vegetables are not fully cooked. Place the vegetables directly from the grill into a bowl, cover with plastic wrap and let sit for 10 minutes. This will finish cooking the veggies. While still warm, toss with the pesto. Adjust the seasoning.

Serve warm or at room temperature. *Serves 6*

TASTE This pesto does have its share of garlic, but the lemon zest gives it a palate-cleansing effect so the pesto won't stay with you all evening.

TECHNIQUE I prefer *not* to brush veggies with oil before I put them on the grill. If the grill is clean, the veggies won't stick, plus raw eggplant will soak up as much oil as you brush onto it before it hits the grill. The vegetables will happily take on flavor when dressed while still a little warm.

TALE In the summer, Michael and I enjoy market vegetables so much that we tend to overbuy because we are so drawn to the selection. Quite often we'll get home from the market, and while we intended to grill a piece of fish or chicken, we just end up digging in and enjoying vegetable after vegetable.

SPINACH, CORN & HERB STUFFED PEPPERS

These stuffed peppers could easily replace the starch component of dinner and be perfect alongside chicken or fish. Or they can be served with a salad for a nice lunch.

1 lb **fresh or frozen spinach leaves** 500 g

6 **red bell peppers**

2 cups **fresh or frozen corn kernels** 500 mL

1 cup **chopped green onion** 250 mL

1 tub **(1 lb/500 g) creamy ricotta cheese**

½ cup **chopped fresh basil** 125 mL

¼ cup **chopped fresh oregano** 60 mL

2 Tbsp **chopped fresh mint** 30 mL

2 tsp **finely grated lime zest** 10 mL

1 Tbsp **fresh lime juice** 15 mL

salt & pepper

If using fresh spinach, blanch spinach in salted boiling water for 30 seconds. Drain, cool and then squeeze out excess liquid. If using frozen, thaw and squeeze out excess liquid. Roughly chop.

Preheat the oven to 375°F (190°C). Cut off the tops of the peppers, removing the seeds and stem but finely dicing the rest of the pepper tops. Place this in a bowl and mix with the corn, green onion and spinach. Stir in the ricotta and add the fresh herbs and lime zest and juice. Season to taste. Spoon the filling into peppers and place in an ungreased baking dish. Cover and bake for 30 minutes, then remove cover and bake 10 minutes more. Serve immediately. *Serves 6*

TASTE You can certainly use low-fat ricotta in this recipe. Actually I find that low-fat ricotta can be safely substituted for regular ricotta in most recipes, even for baking.

TECHNIQUE Use this ricotta filling for vegetable cannelloni or layered into a vegetable lasagne. And now that I think of it, this filling would be great for stuffed tomatoes, which were the original inspiration for this dish.

TALE I do like fresh mint, and I always try to work it into dishes where it makes sense. It is also one of those herbs that grows and grows (even I, who is green thumb–challenged, can grow it), which is another reason why I am looking to use it, just to keep on top of it. Good thing I like it in my iced tea.

BRAISED EDAMAME WITH LEEKS & MISO

Soybeans (or *edamame*) make a healthy and hearty vegetable course that complements any roast or grilled meat, be it chicken, pork or beef.

1 Tbsp **vegetable oil** 15 mL
2 cups **finely chopped leeks, white and light green parts only** 500 mL
2 tsp **finely grated fresh ginger** 10 mL

1 pkg **(1 lb/454 g) frozen shelled edamame (see Taste)**
1 Tbsp **light miso paste (see Taste)** 15 mL
dash **sesame oil**
1 Tbsp **sesame seeds, toasted** 15 mL

Heat a large sauté pan over medium heat and add the oil. Add the leeks and ginger and sauté until tender, about 3 minutes. Add the frozen edamame and 1 cup (250 mL) of water and bring to a simmer. Continue simmering, uncovered, until almost all the liquid has evaporated. Reduce the heat to low and stir in the miso paste and sesame oil. (Miso is salty—seasoning this with salt should not be necessary.) Stir in the sesame seeds and serve.
Serves 4

TASTE *Miso* is fermented soybean paste and can be purchased at many grocery stores, Asian food stores or even health food stores. Light miso has a golden brown color and a milder taste than dark miso. Edamame can be found in the frozen food section of most grocery stores. It is sold both shelled and unshelled.

TECHNIQUE When cooking with miso paste, it should be added at the very end of the cooking time, but with cold dishes it can be added anytime.

TALE Here in the Niagara there are soybean fields everywhere. It grows well in this area and is lucrative for the farmers. When I asked a farmer why I couldn't buy fresh soybeans in the shell at the farmers' market, it was explained to me that the local crops are a different variety that are grown for their oil and unpalatable. I'd love to see some of the edible beans produced here someday.

CHICKPEA PEPPER TOSS

I like to make this dish when I'm in a hurry or when it's really hot out and I don't feel like turning on the stove.

1½ cups **diced roasted red pepper (1-inch/2.5 cm dice)** 375 mL

1 cup **diced red onion (¼-inch/6 mm dice)** 250 mL

2 cans **(14 oz/398 mL) chickpeas, drained and rinsed**

⅔ cup **roughly chopped fresh Italian parsley** 160 mL

2 tsp **finely chopped fresh rosemary** 10 mL

2 tsp **finely grated lemon zest** 10 mL

¼ cup **lemon juice** 60 mL

salt & pepper

Toss all the ingredients together in a large bowl and season to taste. Serve chilled, warmed or at room temperature. *Serves 4 as a main dish, 8 as a side*

TASTE This is one of those anytime-with-anything vegetable courses. It's versatile too—mix with 2 cups (500 mL) of cooked pasta and you've got a nice pasta salad.

TECHNIQUE If you wish to use dried chickpeas for this recipe, start with ¾ cup (190 mL) of dried chickpeas and soak them in cool water for four hours or overnight. Drain and gently simmer them in unsalted water until tender, about 45 minutes.

TALE Another reason I like this dish? Only a knife, a cutting board and a bowl as dishes!

SWEET POTATO WITH ONION & PUMPKIN SEEDS

What a divine combination—I love the toastiness that the pumpkin seeds lend to the roasted sweet potatoes, and the onions just make the whole dish mellow and easy to enjoy.

3 Tbsp **olive oil** 45 mL
2 cups **sliced onion** 500 mL
1 tsp **chopped fresh thyme** 10 mL
1½ lb **sweet potato, peeled and cut into ½-inch (1 cm) dice** 750 g

salt & pepper
2 Tbsp **lemon juice** 30 mL
⅓ cup **unsalted pumpkin seeds, toasted** 80 mL

Preheat the oven to 375°F (190°C). In a medium heavy-bottomed sauté pan, heat the oil over medium heat and add the onions and thyme. Sauté until the onions are caramelized, about 40 minutes (reduce the heat if they are browning too quickly—see Technique on pages 5 and 42). Transfer to a 12½- x 13½-inch (3.5 L) baking dish and toss in the diced sweet potatoes. Season lightly, cover and roast for 30 minutes, or until sweet potatoes are tender. Remove from the oven and stir in the lemon juice and pumpkin seeds, and adjust seasoning if needed. Sweet potatoes can be served warm or at room temperature. *Serves 6*

TASTE The sweetness of sweet potato can sometimes be a bit much, but between the onions, pumpkin seeds and that final splash of lemon juice, the potato is balanced perfectly and is given dimension and character.

TECHNIQUE I peel my sweet potatoes out of personal preference, but you can't deny that the skins are packed with nutrients. Please feel free to keep the skins on.

TALE I pop this onto menus all the time, and it is my new favorite recipe to demonstrate at cooking classes. Its simplicity easily impresses everyone.

MOROCCAN SPICED PARSNIPS As with the Vegetable Tagine (page 139), fragrant spices can bring the best out of vegetables. I like to serve this with lamb or beef dishes.

MOROCCAN SPICE MIX
2 Tbsp **ground cumin** 30 mL
1 Tbsp **ground coriander** 15 mL
1 Tbsp **ground ginger** 15 mL
2 tsp **ground cinnamon** 10 mL
1 tsp **ground black pepper** 5 mL
¼ tsp **ground cloves** 1 mL

THE PARSNIPS
1½ lb **parsnips** 750 g
1 Tbsp **olive oil** 15 mL
2 Tbsp **nut oil such as walnut or almond** 30 mL
2 Tbsp **Morrocan Spice Mix** 30 mL
1 tsp **coarse salt** 5 mL

For the Moroccan Spice Mix, toss all the ingredients together. (This spice mix can be stored in an airtight container for up to a month.)

Preheat the oven to 350°F (180°C).

Peel the parsnips and cut into 3-inch (8 cm) pieces and place in a baking dish. Heat the olive oil and nut oil in a small sauté pan over medium heat. Add 2 Tbsp (30 mL) of the spice mix and stir into the oil, heating for 1 minute. Scrape the mixture over the parsnips, add salt and toss to coat. Cover the dish and bake for 25 to 30 minutes, or until parsnips are tender.

Parsnips can be baked in advance and reheated in the oven to serve. *Serves 6*

TASTE Parsnips inherently have a "baker's cupboard" spice flavor that means adding more spice just enhances this vegetable.

TECHNIQUE To have a good spice blend such as this one on hand enriches everyday cooking. This fragrant blend is nice sprinkled on chicken breasts, pork tenderloin and roasted potatoes. For even greater impact, try toasting whole spices (of the same measure) in a sauté pan over medium heat for two to three minutes, then grinding. This creates a full-bodied, rich spice blend. (However, I do find that the finer texture of preground spices works best here for coating the parsnips.)

TALE I include parsnips in just about every wintry dish: pot roast, stews, hearty soups and even chili. In fact, I'll replace turnips in a recipe with parsnips if I feel it's appropriate (turnips are one of the few vegetables I'm not terribly fond of).

ASPARAGUS WITH AVOCADO WASABI "BUTTER"

I love that asparagus can be enjoyed warm or cold. Avocado puréed with olive oil makes this like a creamy and refreshing version of hollandaise (which is another of my favorite companions to asparagus).

For the avocado wasabi butter, purée the avocado, lemon juice and 3 Tbsp (45 mL) warm water in a blender (or use an immersion blender). Slowly drizzle in the oil while blending, and then add the wasabi paste, if using. Season to taste and set aside or chill until ready to serve.

To prepare the asparagus for cooking, peel them halfway if you like (see Technique) and then trim the stem ends. Bring a pot of water to a boil, and add salt and the asparagus. Cook until the asparagus yields when pierced with a fork, and drain. Serve immediately with the avocado butter spooned on top.

To serve the dish cold (equally delicious), immerse the asparagus in ice water, not only to halt the cooking process and chill the asparagus but also to set the vibrant green color. Chill until ready to serve.

Serves 4

1 **ripe avocado**
2 Tbsp **lemon juice** 30 mL
3 Tbsp **olive oil** 45 mL
1 Tbsp **wasabi paste**
   (optional—see Taste)
   15 mL
salt & pepper
1½ lb **fresh asparagus** 750 g

TASTE I like the sinus-cleansing heat that wasabi paste can add, sort of like our traditional horseradish (wasabi is horseradish, too). It's a heat that makes its presence known but then evaporates, unlike chili pepper heat, which can linger. Look for wasabi paste in Asian food stores.

TECHNIQUE I like to peel the outside of the asparagus halfway for aesthetic reasons—it just looks so nice. But also I end up having to trim less off the bottom because peeling removes the fibrous outer layer that is hard to eat.

TALE I also use this wasabi avocado butter on chicken sandwiches.

BLOODY CAESAR TOMATOES

Need a nice partner for grilled halibut or even a grilled or baked chicken breast? This will become a friend for life.

2 fresh, ripe tomato, cut into wedges

3 Tbsp red wine vinegar 45 mL

1 clove garlic, minced

¼ cup finely diced red onion 60 mL

¼ cup finely diced celery 60 mL

1 Tbsp celery salt 15 mL

1 Tbsp prepared horse-radish 15 mL

3 dashes Worcestershire sauce

dash Tabasco sauce

ground black pepper

Toss the tomato, vinegar and garlic together in a bowl, cover and let sit 30 minutes. Strain the liquid from the tomatoes into a small pot and reduce to 2 Tbsp (30 mL) over medium heat. Add this reduction back to the tomatoes and toss in the remaining ingredients. Season to taste with black pepper and chill until ready to serve. *Makes about 3 cups (750 mL)*

TASTE There are only two Bloody Caesar ingredients lacking in this recipe that you are welcome to add. The first is clam juice (not really recommended in this case), the second is vodka (well, that one is up to you).

TECHNIQUE Reducing the tomato juices intensifies the flavors. This also works for the Tomato Bruschetta Quinoa recipe (page 133) as mentioned in its Technique sidebar. A good trick is worth repeating.

TALE Having a Bloody Caesar cocktail is an indulgence I don't often give myself, but when I do, it *must* have horseradish and an extra dash of Tabasco to make it just right.

[BREAD, BREAKFAST & BEVERAGES]

The three Bs of the kitchen, bread, breakfast and beverages, are like the three Rs in school—they're the basic fundamentals. The three Bs fuel and frame the day, from the first sip of coffee in the morning taken with a bite of a Banana Bran Muffin (page 158), or a soothing glass of Mulled Wine (page 170) in the evening.

When I became a pastry chef, someone told me a great piece of wisdom: "You have a very important role as pastry chef in a restaurant. You give the customers the first taste of their whole dining experience with the bread served before the meal, and the last taste with the dessert. You *frame* the entire experience."

In this chapter I cover some baking basics, and, when it comes to breakfast, I try to make all happy with a range from tasty and decadent to healthy and hearty. It's not easy—I find breakfast the toughest meal to please people with. We are creatures of habit, and never more so than when we first get up, since we're not yet functioning at our full potential.

And a morning ritual or routine can make the day. On a regular weekday, mine starts first with coffee, while I get myself ready for the world. Then, if I'm good (and I try to be), I'll have some oatmeal to start the day. Weekends and/or days off are for hot breakfasts, when there's more time for experimenting and baking. Baked goods like muffins and coffee cake are not only great for breakfast, but also make for a nice tea break.

PARKER HOUSE ROLLS

Parker House rolls are known for being buttery and tender. This is not artisanal bread baking. This is meant to go with comfort food, or become a minisandwich with leftover roast beef or chicken.

Stir the yeast, milk and sugar into the tepid water in a large bowl, or in the bowl of a stand mixer fitted with a dough hook, and let sit 5 minutes. Stir in the egg, 3 cups (750 mL) of flour and salt, then 2 Tbsp (30 mL) melted butter. Mix dough until it just comes together (on low speed if using a mixer), adding more flour if it's too sticky. Increase the speed 1 level higher than low and mix for 3 minutes, or turn the dough out onto a lightly floured work surface and knead for 5 minutes. Place the dough in a lightly greased bowl, cover with plastic wrap and let rise in a warm, draught-free place until doubled in size, about 1½ hours.

Preheat the oven to 375°F (190°C) and brush a 9- x 13-inch (3.5 L) pan with some of the melted butter.

Turn risen dough out onto a lightly floured surface, knead lightly and roll to an 18-inch (45 cm) square about ¼-inch (6 mm) thick. Slice the dough into 36 squares (cut each way by 6) and brush the surface of the dough with melted butter. Use the back of a butter knife to fold each square in half and place in the buttered pan with the fold facing up, leaving only ½-inch (1 cm) space in between each roll. Butter the tops of the rolls and cover loosely with plastic wrap. Let sit for 15 minutes. Remove the wrap and bake for about 15 minutes, or until the rolls are golden brown. Let rolls cool on a wire rack for 10 minutes before serving. *Makes about 3 dozen*

1½ Tbsp **instant yeast** 23 mL
1 cup **2% milk, at room temperature** 250 mL
1 Tbsp **sugar** 15 mL
¼ cup **tepid water (about 105°F/41°C)** 60 mL
1 **large egg**
3–3½ cups **all-purpose flour** 750–875 mL
1 tsp **fine salt** 5 mL
½ cup **unsalted butter, melted** 125 mL

TASTE The milk in this recipe contributes to the soft, fine texture of these rolls. Many store-bought rolls use skim milk powder (not a dishonorable trait) to accomplish this same effect.

TECHNIQUE Don't be afraid to get physical with your bread dough. Whether kneading or rolling out, your dough can take the workout. The moment it starts rebelling and springing back on you then you know it's hit its peak. Now it just needs time to rest.

TALE I make these rolls on Michael's request. Michael's mom used to make them, so they are like comfort food to him.

CRANBERRY ORANGE SCONES These are
the flaky, not-too-sweet style of scone that I favor with a cup of tea.

1½ cups **all-purpose flour**
375 mL

3 Tbsp **sugar** 45 mL

1½ tsp **baking powder**
7.5 mL

1 Tbsp **finely grated orange
zest** 15 mL

¼ tsp **fine salt** 1 mL

6 Tbsp **unsalted butter, cut
into pieces and chilled**
90 mL

½ cup **half-and-half cream
(10%), plus extra for
brushing** 125 mL

⅔ cup **dried cranberries**
160 mL

Preheat the oven to 375°F (190°C). Grease a baking sheet or line it with
parchment paper.

Place the flour, sugar, baking powder and orange zest in a mixing bowl,
or in the bowl of a stand mixer fitted with the paddle attachment. Cut the
butter into the dry ingredients until it resembles coarse meal, and then add
the cream. Mix just until dough comes together. Stir in the cranberries.

Turn dough onto a lightly floured surface. Roll out the dough to an inch
(2.5 cm) thick, fold in half and repeat again (this is the secret to a flaky
scone). Roll out the dough a third time to a disc 1 inch (2.5 cm) thick and cut
into 6 wedges. Place on the prepared baking sheet and brush with remaining cream. Bake for 15 to 18 minutes, or until tops are nicely browned.

Makes 6 scones

TASTE These scones have the ability to take on different personalities depending on the
occasion. They are festive enough to suit a holiday breakfast, common and simple enough for
a Tuesday tea break and delicate enough to serve at brunch with company.

TECHNIQUE Ah, my secret to a flaky scone—the folding while rolling. I figure that if
puff pastry benefits by rolling out and folding, then a scone can do just as well with the same
technique.

TALE If I forget to eat lunch because I get busy, I'm inclined to grab one of these scones, slice
it in half and put in a slice or two of cheddar. Now that's an easy snack.

PHOTO Cranberry Orange
Scones *served with* Perfect Iced Tea
(page 168)

BEST BANANA BRAN MUFFINS

Bran muffins are notorious for being not only high in fiber but high in fat as well. By adding the moisture of mashed ripe banana, I can keep the fat content down to a minimum.

1½ cups **wheat bran** 375 mL
1 cup **buttermilk** 250 mL
1½ cups **mashed ripe banana (about 2 or 3)** 375 mL
⅔ cup **light brown sugar, packed** 160 mL
2 **large eggs**

¼ cup **vegetable oil** 60 mL
1½ cups **all-purpose flour** 375 mL
1¼ tsp **baking powder** 6 mL
½ **tsp fine salt** 2 mL
½ **tsp ground cinnamon** 2 mL
½ cup **raisins** 125 mL

Preheat the oven to 350°F (180°C) and grease a 12-cup muffin tin. In a small bowl stir the bran and buttermilk to blend and let sit for 15 minutes. In a large bowl, whisk the banana, sugar, eggs and oil to blend. Stir the bran mixture into banana mixture. In a separate bowl, stir the flour, baking powder, salt and cinnamon, and add to the batter, stirring just until combined (a few lumps are fine). Stir in raisins and spoon into the prepared muffin tin. Bake for 20 to 25 minutes, or until the top of a muffin springs back when pressed. Cool for 15 minutes in the tin before turning out on a wire rack to cool completely.

Muffins will keep in an airtight container for up to 4 days, or frozen for up to 3 months. *Makes 12 muffins*

TASTE   I like to let the bran soak in the buttermilk to let it plump up. This makes for a tender muffin that you're not chewing on like a cow chews its cud.

TECHNIQUE   The technique for most muffins is called the "quick bread" method. You combine the wet ingredients in one bowl, the dry ingredients in another, and then quickly blend the two. The method comes by its name earnestly.

TALE   All right, I may have managed to reduce the fat in these muffins, but my favorite way to eat them is still warm from the oven and slathered with butter or cream cheese.

HERMIT COFFEE CAKE

I love hermit cookies packed with dried fruits and nuts. I also love date and raisin loaf. So I decided to meld the best of both worlds and create this coffee cake concoction.

1½ cups **chopped pitted dates** 375 mL	½ tsp **baking powder** 2 mL
1 cup **orange juice** 250 mL	¼ tsp **fine salt** 1 mL
1½ cups **all-purpose flour** 375 mL	¼ tsp **ground cloves** 1 mL
½ cup **sugar** 125 mL	1 **large egg**
1 tsp **baking soda** 5 mL	¼ cup **vegetable oil** 60 mL
	¾ cup **golden raisins** 190 mL
	¾ cup **walnut pieces** 190 mL

Preheat the oven to 350°F (180°C). Grease a 9-inch (2.5 L) square pan.

In a small saucepan over medium-low heat, bring the dates and orange juice up to a simmer. Remove from the heat and let cool to room temperature. In a large bowl, sift the flour, sugar, baking soda, baking powder, salt and cloves. In a separate bowl, whisk together the egg and oil. Add the egg mixture and dates to the flour mixture and stir just until blended. Stir in the raisins and walnuts. Scrape into the prepared pan and bake for about 45 minutes, or until a tester inserted in the center of the cake comes out clean. Let the cake cool in the pan for 10 minutes, then turn out on a wire rack to cool completely. *Makes one 9-inch (2.5 L) square pan*

TASTE I normally don't favor nuts in my coffee cakes—I even prefer raisins in my carrot cake over walnuts—but there's something inherently right about walnuts in this cake. They're so tender and mild, they match the texture of the coffee cake perfectly.

TECHNIQUE Soaking the dates in the orange juice is the same technique I use for sticky toffee pudding, so they are more thoroughly incorporated into the batter as opposed to being a distinct ingredient like a raisin or nut. There's no reason why that same technique can't be applied here!

TALE I was testing a number of coffee cake recipes when I first made this at home. I knew this was a winner because when I went back to the plate of all the different samples that I left for others to try, there were none left of this one. Taste is the best judge.

CARROT ORANGE LOAF

I've kept this loaf very simple. It's perfect for a tea or coffee break or after dinner, those times when you want a little something sweet (but not too sweet).

½ cup **vegetable oil** 125 mL
1 cup **sugar** 250 mL
1 **large egg**
1 cup **finely shredded carrot** 250 mL
½ tsp **finely grated orange zest** 2 mL

1½ cup **all-purpose flour** 375 mL
½ tsp **baking soda** 2 mL
½ tsp **baking powder** 2 mL
1 tsp **ground cinnamon** 5 mL
½ tsp **ground nutmeg** 2 mL
½ tsp **fine salt** 2 mL

Preheat the oven to 350°F (180°C) and grease a loaf pan.

Whisk the oil, sugar and egg in a large bowl to blend. Stir in the shredded carrot and orange zest. In a separate bowl, sift the flour with baking soda, baking powder, cinnamon, nutmeg and salt. Stir the flour mixture into the carrot mixture and stir just until blended. Scrape into the prepared pan and bake for 55 to 60 minutes, or until a tester inserted in the center of the cake comes out clean. Cool in the pan for 10 minutes, then turn the loaf out onto a plate to cool completely. *Makes one 8½- x 4½-inch (1.5 L) loaf*

TASTE Just like a good carrot cake, you could add ¾ cup (190 mL) of raisins or walnut pieces, depending on your preference.

TECHNIQUE To turn this into a more formal dessert cake, double this recipe and bake in two 8-inch (20 cm) round cake pans. They'll take only about 40 minutes to bake. Make your favorite cream cheese icing recipe, stack the two layers with icing in between and all around, and voilà: you've got a birthday cake.

TALE I turn this recipe to a zucchini loaf by replacing the grated carrot with the same measure of zucchini—and then I also like to add ½ cup (125 mL) chocolate chips.

BUTTERMILK BLUEBERRY PANCAKES
Weekends or days off are for hot breakfasts, served leisurely in comfy clothes and slippers.

1 cup **all-purpose flour** 250 mL

2 Tbsp **cornmeal** 30 mL

1 tsp **baking powder** 5 mL

1 tsp **baking soda** 5 mL

½ tsp **fine salt** 2 mL

pinch **ground nutmeg**

2 cups **buttermilk** 500 mL

1 **large egg**

2 Tbsp **unsalted butter, melted** 30 mL

2 Tbsp **honey** 30 mL

vegetable oil, for greasing

1½ cups **fresh or frozen blueberries** 375 mL

TO SERVE

butter

maple syrup

Sift the flour, cornmeal, baking powder, baking soda, salt and nutmeg into a large bowl. In a separate bowl, whisk the buttermilk, egg, melted butter and honey to blend. Add the buttermilk mixture to the flour and stir gently just until combined (a few lumps are fine).

Preheat the oven to 200°F (95°C). Heat a griddle over medium heat and grease lightly with vegetable oil. Ladle a ¼ cup (60 mL) of batter for each pancake onto the griddle and sprinkle with blueberries. Cook for about 3 minutes (see Technique), then flip and cook another 2 to 3 minutes until done. Remove the pancakes to a plate and keep covered and warm in the oven while preparing the remaining pancakes.

Serve pancakes with butter and maple syrup. *Serves 4*

TASTE I often substitute bananas for the blueberries and stir a dash of cinnamon into the batter. And switch these into oatmeal pancakes by decreasing the flour to ½ cup (125 mL) and soaking ½ cup (125 mL) oatmeal in the buttermilk for ten minutes before blending.

TECHNIQUE The batter starts off shiny, but will take on a dull finish after a few minutes in the pan—that's when you know it's ready to flip. And no need to push the blueberries (or bananas) into the pancake, as they settle into place on their own

TALE It's a nice gesture to serve the maple syrup warmed on the side. It's so much nicer after buttering your pancakes to pour warm maple syrup over the stack.

ANNA'S FAVORITE OATMEAL

I love my oatmeal. You can put whatever you like on yours, but I'm giving you a list of what I like on mine. This is my morning routine.

pinch **fine salt**
1 cup **rolled oats (not quick-cooking)** 250 mL
3 Tbsp **oat bran** 45 mL

TOPPINGS
brown sugar
golden raisins
ground cinnamon
2% milk

Bring 2½ cups (625 mL) of water just up to a boil in a medium saucepan. Add salt and stir in the oatmeal and oat bran. Reduce the heat to low, cover and simmer slowly for 20 minutes, stirring occasionally.

Spoon the oatmeal into bowls and finish with toppings. *Serves 4*

TASTE A good bowl of oatmeal is as much about the texture as it is about the toppings. I like regular oats because they don't become soggy like quick or instant tends to. And forgive me, but I find that steel cut oats are just too much work (and take a fair bit longer to cook).

TECHNIQUE I picked up the trick with the oat bran from my sister-in-law, Linda. By adding oat bran to the pot, it comes out not only higher in fiber, but über-fluffy. You'll be amazed!

TALE There's something inherently satisfying about a good bowl of oatmeal in the morning. It's kind of like the first day of school—everyone starts the year with an A average. With a bowl of oatmeal to start your day, all the indulgences later on that day count for less.

2IST CENTURY GRANOLA

If I can't get my oatmeal in the morning, then give me granola. It challenges the palate and the texture is fabulous, whether softened by milk or yogurt or crunchy when snacked on in the car on the way to work.

1 cup **wheat berries (wheat kernels)** 250 mL	⅔ cup **maple syrup** 160 mL
3 cups **rolled oats** 750 mL	3 Tbsp **vegetable oil** 45 mL
½ cup **rolled barley or spelt flakes** 125 mL	1½ tsp **ground cinnamon** 7.5 mL
3 Tbsp **millet** 45 mL	¾ tsp **fine salt** 4 mL
¾ cup **whole almonds** 190 mL	¾ tsp **ground cardamom** 4 mL
¾ cup **whole hazelnuts** 190 mL	¼ tsp **ground nutmeg** 1 mL
3 Tbsp **unsalted pumpkin seeds** 45 mL	¾ cup **golden raisins** 190 mL
3 Tbsp **unsalted sunflower seeds** 45 mL	½ cup **dried cranberries** 125 mL
2 Tbsp **sesame seeds** 30 mL	½ cup **chopped pitted dates** 125 mL
	½ cup **chopped dried apricots** 125 mL

Cook wheat berries in salted boiling water for 1 hour. Alternately wheat berries can be soaked in cold water overnight, then cooked for 30 to 40 minutes until tender. Drain and rinse to cool.

Preheat the oven to 350°F (180°C) and line a baking sheet with parchment paper.

In a large bowl toss the cooled wheat berries with the oats, barley or spelt flakes, millet, nuts and seeds. In a separate bowl, whisk the maple syrup, oil, cinnamon, salt, cardamom and nutmeg. Pour the maple mixture over the grains and stir well to coat. Spread the granola evenly on the prepared baking sheet and bake for about 25 minutes, stirring occasionally, until granola is richly browned. Let cool for 20 minutes in the baking sheet on a wire rack.

After the granola has cooled but is still warm to the touch, break it into pieces and toss with the dried fruits.

Granola will keep up to 2 weeks in an airtight container. *Makes about 8 cups (2 L)*

TASTE Wheat berries are my contemporary addition to this granola. Whole grains rock, and toasting cooked wheat kernels (more appetizingly known as wheat berries) add a new crunch to granola.

TECHNIQUE Dried fruits need to be added *after* the granola has come out of the oven or else they would burn if baked with everything else. But add them before the granola cools completely so that the fruit can adhere to all the other goodies.

TALE I know this looks like a long list of ingredients for "just" granola, but it's really not a lot of work, just a complex melding of flavors and textures that is pure magic.

REALLY GOOD GRANOLA BARS

These are a tender, soft style of granola bar that is a lot more gratifying and a lot healthier than the store-bought kind. (Have you read the ingredients on a box of granola bars lately?)

2 cups **rolled oats (not quick-cooking)** 500 mL

1 cup **chopped peanuts** 250 mL

½ cup **shredded coconut, sweetened or unsweetened** 125 mL

½ cup **raisins** 125 mL

¼ cup **unsalted sunflower seeds** 60 mL

¼ cup **unsalted pumpkin seeds** 60 mL

1 cup **peanut butter** 250 mL

1 cup **light brown sugar, packed** 250 mL

5 Tbsp **unsalted butter** 75 mL

2 tsp **vanilla extract** 10 mL

1 tsp **ground cinnamon** 5 mL

½ tsp **ground nutmeg** 2 mL

½ tsp **fine salt** 2 mL

1 **large egg**

Preheat the oven to 350°F (180°C). Grease and line a 9-inch (2.5 L) square pan with parchment paper so that the paper hangs over the sides of the pan.

Toss the oats, peanuts, coconut, raisins and sunflower and pumpkin seeds together in a bowl. In a pot over medium-low heat, stir together the peanut butter, brown sugar, butter, vanilla, cinnamon, nutmeg and salt until melted. Pour this over the oat mixture and stir until blended. Stir in the egg. Spread the granola into the prepared pan, patting down to make even. Bake for 30 minutes, then cool to room temperature before chilling in the fridge for 2 hours.

To cut, lift the granola out of pan with parchment paper and cut into 24 to 30 bars. *Makes one 9-inch (2.5 L) square pan (24 to 30 bars)*

TASTE This granola bar recipe has a little bit of everything in it, and worthy of note is how the texture of all the ingredients is consistent. Peanuts, sunflower seeds and pumpkin seeds are all soft and tender, making the granola bars easy to slice and easy to eat.

TECHNIQUE I recommend using pure, unsweetened peanut butter in this recipe. You can also substitute another nut or seed butter if you wish.

TALE I love coconut, so I tend to sneak it in wherever I can— for example, try adding 1 cup (250 mL) of coconut to the granola recipe on the facing page. My favorite place to sneak in shredded coconut? Chocolate brownies!

HUEVOS RANCHEROS
These "rancher's eggs" are a big hit at our house. If I owned a breakfast place (maybe someday, you never know), this would be a regular feature on the menu.

RANCHEROS MIX
4 slices **bacon, diced**
1 cup **diced onion** 250 mL
½ cup **diced red pepper** 125 mL
1 cup **fresh corn off the cob** 250 mL
1 clove **garlic, minced**
1 **jalapeño pepper, seeded and finely chopped**
2 tsp **ground cumin** 10 mL

2 tsp **ground coriander** 10 mL
1 can **(14 oz/398 mL) black beans, drained and rinsed**
1 cup **diced fresh tomato** 250 mL
3 Tbsp **chopped fresh cilantro (more for garnish)** 45 mL
salt & pepper

HUEVOS
6 **small flour tortillas**
2 cups **grated cheddar cheese** 500 mL
12 **eggs**
salt & pepper
sour cream, for garnish
chopped fresh cilantro, for garnish

For the rancheros mix, heat a large sauté pan over medium heat and add the bacon. Cook until crisp, remove from the pan and set aside. Drain all but 1 Tbsp (15 mL) of the bacon drippings. Add the onion and red pepper to the drippings and sauté over medium heat until onions are translucent, about 5 minutes. Stir in the corn, garlic, jalapeño and ground cumin and coriander and cook for 2 minutes. Add the beans and tomato and cook until warmed through. Remove from the heat, stir in the cilantro and season to taste.

Preheat the oven to 400°F (200°C). Grease six 8 oz (228 mL) ovenproof dishes and line each with a tortilla. Spoon the ranchero mix into each tortilla and sprinkle with grated cheddar. Break 2 eggs into each dish and season lightly. Bake for 15 minutes, or until the eggs are of desired doneness. Place each dish on a saucer (be careful—the dishes will be hot), and top with a spoonful of sour cream and a sprinkle of the fresh cilantro and reserved bacon and serve immediately. *Serves 6*

TASTE It's fantastic how the ingredients and flavors of a Mexican-inspired lunch or dinner can easily be adapted to breakfast just by serving eggs on top.

TECHNIQUE Typically, huevos rancheros are served baked on a flat tortilla, but I like serving the eggs baked in twos in individual large dishes. You can also try a single egg baked into a muffin cup.

TALE I first tried huevos rancheros on a visit to Santa Fe, New Mexico. The brunch spot was known for its sticky buns, which I found didn't compare to the fabulous egg dish.

SPICED ICED COFFEE
Refreshing on a hot day, this spiced coffee makes great use of an unfinished morning pot of brew.

4 shots **espresso coffee**

3 Tbsp **dark brown sugar, packed** 45 mL

2 **cinnamon sticks**

2 **whole star anise**

3 **whole green cardamom pods**

3 **whole black peppercorns**

3 cups **2% milk** 750 mL

ice

Stir 1 cup (250 mL) of water, coffee and brown sugar in a saucepan over low heat. Break cinnamon sticks in half and add. Crush the star anise, cardamom pods and peppercorns and add. Keep warm, just below a simmer for 15 minutes. Strain out the spices and stir the coffee mixture with the milk. Pour over ice and serve. *Makes about 4 cups (1 L)*

TASTE If you can't use espresso shots, 1½ cups (375 mL) of regular, strongly brewed coffee works fine—just skip adding the additional water.

TECHNIQUE The coffee used in this recipe is intentionally strong because the ice, as it melts, will dilute it to a perfect balance of spicy and cold.

TALE Michael learned how to make great chai tea from culinary students of his who were Indian. I took this respected technique and applied it gratifyingly to what is now a favorite around our house.

PERFECT ICED TEA I love my iced tea. In the summertime I always have a pitcher of homemade iced tea in my fridge.

2 **tea bags (black, green or herbal)**

TO GARNISH (OPTIONAL)
sugar or honey
citrus slices
mint
berries
sliced peaches
sliced cucumber

Bring 2 cups (500 mL) water up to a full roiling boil. Pour the water over the tea bags in a pitcher (see Technique) and let sit, without stirring, until cooled to room temperature. Remove the tea bags without squeezing and add 2 cups (500 mL) cold water. Sweeten and garnish as desired and serve over plenty of ice. *Makes 4 cups (1 L)*

TASTE By not squeezing out the tea bags you guarantee that your iced tea won't have any bitterness to it.

TECHNIQUE If you are making your iced tea in a glass or ceramic pitcher, be sure to pour the water over a metal spoon placed in the pitcher. The spoon will absorb the impact of the heat and prevent the pitcher from cracking.

TALE I had never seen so much iced tea consumed as I did when I worked in Texas. The restaurant I worked at served iced tea by the 16-ounce (500 mL) glass, and customers would have three and four glasses before the end of a meal. And I thought *I* liked iced tea!

MINT LIMEADE

If you order a mojito at a bar, they muddle the mint in the bottom of a glass with sugar, add lime juice and then rum and ice. This version keeps it family friendly, but feel free to add rum after the kids go down for their nap.

Bring 2½ cups (625 mL) water, the sugar and the mint slowly up to a simmer over medium-low heat. As soon as it simmers, remove the pot from the heat, strain and let cool to room temperature. Stir in the lime juice and serve over ice, garnished with fresh mint. *Makes 4 cups (1 L)*

1¼ cups **sugar** 310 mL
1 bunch **fresh mint, about ¾ cup (190 mL) loosely packed, plus extra for garnish**
1 cup **fresh lime juice** 250 mL

TASTE Give me the choice between limeade and lemonade and I'll always pick limeade. There's a delicate taste to limeade that seems a little more refined than lemonade, and fresh mint just serves to highlight this.

TECHNIQUE It's important to let this simple sugar syrup cool completely before adding the lime juice. By adding the juice to a cooled syrup, you retain all that fresh flavor—very refreshing.

TALE I try and do my part when it comes to culinary research, and test local mojitos wherever I am on vacation. The sacrifices of the job are endless . . .

MULLED WINE A lovely welcome to guests visiting after a wintry drive to your house is the warming scent of mulling wine.

1 bottle **full-bodied red wine, such as Cabernet Sauvignon or Shiraz (3 cups/750 mL)**

1 cup **clear nonalcoholic apple cider or cranberry juice** 250 mL

¼ cup **honey** 60 mL

2 sprigs **fresh rosemary, plus extra for garnish**

3 **cinnamon sticks**

3 **whole star anise**

3 **whole cloves**

3 **whole peppercorns**

1 **orange, sliced**

2 oz **brandy (optional)** 60 mL

In a large pot, slowly bring all the ingredients except the brandy to just below a simmer over medium-low heat. Keep just below a simmer for 20 minutes, then stir in the brandy (if using). Serve, garnishing each wine glass with a sprig of rosemary. *Makes 4 cups (1 L) • Serves 4 to 6*

TASTE Using fresh rosemary is my little festive twist to mulled wine. It may not be expected, but it truly works with the other spices, and a sprig in the glass makes an appropriate garnish.

TECHNIQUE When mulling wine, be sure to keep the wine just below a simmer so that you don't boil away the alcohol. I do recommend using the brandy, but add it right before serving. Since the wine never reaches a simmer, serving it in wine glasses should be fine—just not your Riedel crystal!

TALE You can make a family-friendly version of mulled cider—follow the recipe exactly except use all apple cider instead.

[SWEET TREATS & DESSERTS]

I have such a strong relationship with baking that I could hardly include fewer recipes. It is difficult to narrow down what I like to just one chapter.

Since I like to bake based on my cravings, I provide a few recipes for every type of sweet. Sometimes what I want is just a little cookie, or perhaps I have the time and inclination for a grand torte, or a nice fruit tart can hit the spot—especially when berries are in season.

When I decide to bake something sweet at home, the first thing I always do is look in the fridge to make sure I have enough milk—not necessarily for the recipe, but because I know I'll want a big glass with whatever I am baking.

CHEWY OATMEAL NUGGETS
I like to keep my chocolate chip cookies simple and add nothing more than chocolate chips, but oatmeal cookies are different. I'll stir in a little bit of everything I have in my baker's cupboard. The combination of dark brown sugar (which is very moist) and honey is your guarantee that you cookies will be chewy.

½ cup **unsalted butter, at room temperature** 125 mL
1 cup **dark brown sugar, packed** 250 mL
½ cup **honey** 125 mL
2 **large eggs**
1 tsp **finely grated orange zest** 5 mL
2 cups **all-purpose flour** 500 mL

1 tsp **baking soda** 5 mL
1 tsp **ground cinnamon** 5 mL
½ tsp **ground ginger** 2 mL
¼ tsp **ground nutmeg** 1 mL
1 cup **rolled oats** 250 mL
1 cup **raisins** 250 mL
1 cup **chopped pitted dates** 250 mL
¼ cup **chopped walnut pieces** 60 mL

Preheat the oven to 325°F (160°C) and line 2 baking sheets with parchment paper.

Cream the butter, brown sugar and honey in a large bowl until smooth. Add the eggs and orange zest and beat well. In a separate bowl, combine the flour, baking soda and spices. Stir into the butter mixture to combine. Stir in the oats, then add the raisins, dates and walnut pieces. Drop by tablespoonfuls (15 mL) onto the prepared baking sheet 2 inches (5 cm) apart and bake 1 sheet at a time for 18 to 20 minutes, or until slightly browned.

Makes about 2 dozen

TASTE These are superchewy, packed-with-good-stuff cookies. Switch the raisins, dates and walnuts with whatever favorites you may have: white chocolate chips, dried cranberries, sliced almonds, hazelnuts—it's totally up to you.

TECHNIQUE In all my years of baking, I've never bothered to transfer cookies to a wire rack to cool. I find it easiest to cool cookies on the cookie sheet—and also, you're not moving them while they are fragile. The carry-over heat on a baking sheet is virtually nil—the pan cools so quickly that it doesn't impact the cookies.

TALE While I may pretend I am making these for Michael or for company coming over, I'm usually making them for myself.

GIANT PEANUT BUTTER & JELLY THUMBPRINT COOKIES

These are great peanut butter cookies all on their own, but they sure are cute when filled with grape jelly.

1 cup **unsalted butter, at room temperature** 250 mL	1 tsp **vanilla extract** 5 mL
1 cup **sugar** 250 mL	3¾ cups **all-purpose flour** 940 mL
1 cup **light brown sugar, packed** 250 mL	2 tsp **baking powder** 10 mL
1 cup **peanut butter** 250 mL	¼ tsp **baking soda** 1 mL
2 **large eggs**	1 cup **grape jelly or straw-berry or raspberry jam** 250 mL
2 Tbsp **sour cream** 30 mL	

Preheat the oven to 350°F (180°C) and line 2 baking sheets with parchment paper.

In a large bowl, cream the butter, sugar and brown sugar until smooth. Beat in the peanut butter and add eggs, 1 at a time. Stir in the sour cream and vanilla. In a separate bowl, stir the flour, baking powder and baking soda. Add the flour mixture to the peanut butter mixture, stirring to blend. Scoop large tablespoonfuls of dough, shape into a ball and place at least 2 inches (5 cm) apart on each baking sheet. Press an indent in the center of each cookie with your thumb. Bake cookies for 12 to 15 minutes, or until lightly browned, then cool completely before filling indentations with jam.

Makes about 3 dozen large cookies

TASTE This recipe makes 36 GIANT cookies or 48 normal-sized cookies. I also like making small and dainty thumbprint cookies as petit fours for after a fancy meal.

TECHNIQUE I figured that a good peanut butter cookie recipe could work well as a thumbprint cookie, since typically you press down peanut butter cookies with a fork and the indentations remain. When you press your thumb into the cookie, it creates a little space where the jam goes.

TALE I grew up loving my mom's thumbprint cookies—she would always roll them in walnuts and fill them with apricot jam. A holiday cookie tin wasn't complete without them.

PHOTO Clockwise from top left: Chocolate Almond Toffee Bars (page 180), Balance Cookies (page 178), Giant Peanut Butter & Jelly Thumbprint Cookies (this page), Chocolate Prune Rugelach (page 179)

BALANCE COOKIES

These cookies are gluten free, egg free and dairy free. At the same time, they are also tender and tasty.

2 cups **brown rice flour (see Taste)** 500 mL

1 cup **ground almonds** 250 mL

3 Tbsp **sesame seeds, lightly toasted** 45 mL

½ tsp **ground cinnamon** 2 mL

¼ tsp **fine salt** 1 mL

⅓ cup **honey** 80 mL

¼ cup **vegetable oil** 60 mL

whole almonds, for garnish

Preheat the oven to 350°F (180°C) and line 2 baking sheets with parchment paper.

Stir the rice flour, ground almonds, sesame seeds, cinnamon and salt in a large bowl to combine. In a separate bowl, whisk the honey and vegetable oil, and add to the rice flour mixture and blend. Scoop tablespoonfuls (15 mL) of dough and using your hands shape each into a ball, placing 2 inches (5 cm) apart on the prepared baking sheets. Press each cookie to flatten and press a whole almond into the center of each. Bake 1 sheet at a time for about 15 minutes, or until cookies start to brown a little on the bottom. *Makes about 2 dozen cookies*

TASTE The nuttiness of the almonds in these cookies is enhanced by the toasted sesame seeds. Not a typical ingredient for sweets, I sneak sesame seeds into a lot of desserts such as in coffee cakes. Brown rice flour can be purchased at health food stores or often at bulk stores.

TECHNIQUE Because these cookies lack refined sugar, eggs and dairy, their texture may seem a little drier than a typical cookie dough (though the dough isn't at all crumbly) and the cookies will spread only a little, but not too much. After shaping the dough into balls, press the cookies down to the flatness you prefer.

TALE I started making these regularly for the owner of a fitness club, but they became so popular I had to make them for sale just outside the gym.

CHOCOLATE PRUNE RUGELACH

The combination of prune and chocolate may seem unusual, but the two contrasting tastes and textures complement each other beautifully in this cookie.

1 cup **unsalted butter, at room temperature** 250 mL
8 oz **cream cheese, at room temperature** 250 g
2 Tbsp **sugar** 30 mL
¼ tsp **ground nutmeg** 1 mL
¼ tsp **fine salt** 1 mL
3 cups **all-purpose flour** 750 mL

1 cup **loosely packed chopped prunes** 250 mL
1 cup **chocolate chips or coarsely chopped chocolate** 250 mL
2 Tbsp **sugar** 30 mL
¼ tsp **ground cinnamon** 1 mL

1 **large egg whisked with** 2 Tbsp (30 mL) **water, for brushing**
sugar, for sprinkling
icing sugar, for dusting

Beat the butter and cream cheese using an electric hand mixer until fluffy. Add the sugar, nutmeg and salt and blend. Stir in the flour to combine. Shape dough into 4 discs, wrap and chill for at least an hour.

For the filling, pulse the prunes, chocolate, sugar and cinnamon in a food processor until moist.

To assemble, preheat the oven to 350°F (180°C) and line 2 baking sheets with parchment paper. On a lightly floured surface roll out 1 disc in a circle about 8 inches (20 cm) in diameter. Cut dough into 12 triangle wedges, trimming the outside to make a straight edge. Place a teaspoonful (5 mL) of filling at wide end of each triangle. Roll up each cookie into a croissant shape, bending gently to bring the ends together. Repeat with the remaining dough, and arrange 1 inch (2.5 cm) apart on prepared baking sheets. Brush cookies with egg wash and sprinkle with sugar. Bake for about 20 minutes, or until a light brown. Let cool, then dust with icing sugar.

Cookies will keep up to a week in an airtight container, or can be frozen for up to 2 months. *Makes about 4 dozen cookies*

TASTE It's the sweetness of prunes that stands out in these cookies. The cookie dough itself has little sugar. This same sweetness also brings out the good qualities in the chocolate.

TECHNIQUE This cookie dough recipe can also double as a good tart crust for sweet desserts like pecan pie.

TALE When I make cookies for holiday time, I prefer to make the doughs ahead of time, freeze them and then shape and bake the cookies when I need them. This rugelach recipe, though, freezes very nicely *after* they've been baked. In fact, I like the way the cookie softens just a touch once frozen and thawed.

CHOCOLATE ALMOND TOFFEE BARS

This recipe is one of my most requested, so I'm happy to include it in this book.

1½ cups **rolled oats** 375 mL
½ cup **graham cracker crumbs** 125 mL
¼ tsp **fine salt** 1 mL
½ cup **unsalted butter, melted** 125 mL

1 cup **Skor toffee bits** 250 mL
1 cup **chocolate chips** 250 mL
1 cup **sliced almonds** 250 mL
1 can **(9½ oz/300 mL) sweet-ened condensed milk**

Preheat the oven to 350°F (180°C). Grease and line an 8-inch (2 L) square pan with parchment paper so that the paper hangs over the sides of the pan.

Stir the oats, graham cracker crumbs and salt in a bowl to combine, then stir in the melted butter. Press the crumbly oat mixture into the prepared pan. Sprinkle Skor bits evenly on top, followed by chocolate chips and sliced almonds. Pour condensed milk evenly over pan (it will sink in as it bakes) and bake for 30 to 40 minutes, or until the top is golden brown and the edges are bubbling. Cool to room temperature in the pan, then chill for at least 4 hours before slicing into bars.

Store toffee bars in the refrigerator for up to a week. *Makes one 8-inch (2 L) square pan (25 squares)*

TASTE This is decadence in a pan. The sinful combination of chocolate, toffee and almonds enveloped in condensed milk that caramelizes as it bakes is irresistible. At least these have oats in them to redeem themselves, just a little bit.

TECHNIQUE This is a simple recipe to execute—you gather the ingredients and layer them, basically. The challenge is in waiting for them to cool after they've finished baking!

TALE My head pastry chef at Olson Foods + Bakery, Andrea, brought this recipe to my attention. She is an excellent baker, and we go way back. She started with me as a high school co-op student, while I was just picking up professional baking myself on the job, so we learned together. That was about 15 years ago, and after her stint at cooking school and gaining other work experience, I'm thrilled that we are working together again after all these years.

MOCHA HAZELNUT CHEESECAKE This

cheesecake is just like those Ferrero Rocher candies we all love.

CRUST

1 cup **graham cracker crumbs** 250 mL

⅓ cup **ground hazelnuts** 80 mL

¼ cup **light brown sugar, packed** 60 mL

¼ cup **unsalted butter, melted** 60 mL

½ tsp **vanilla extract** 2 mL

FILLING

6 oz **semisweet chocolate, chopped** 175 g

2 cups **whipping cream (35%)** 500 mL

1 Tbsp **instant coffee granules** 15 mL

1 lb **cream cheese, at room temperature** 500 g

¾ cup **sugar** 190 mL

1 Tbsp **cornstarch** 15 mL

½ cup **hazelnut liqueur** 125 mL

2 **large eggs**

cocoa powder, for dusting

whole, toasted and peeled hazelnuts, for garnish (see Technique)

For the crust, preheat the oven to 350°F (180°C) and grease a 9-inch (2.5 L) springform pan. Pulse the crumbs, hazelnuts and brown sugar in a food processor. Add the melted butter and vanilla extract and pulse until it's an even texture. Press into the bottom of the prepared pan and bake for 7 minutes. Allow to cool while preparing filling.

Reduce the oven temperature to 325°F (160°C). For the filling, place the chopped chocolate in a bowl and heat the cream and instant coffee until just before it comes to a simmer. Pour the hot cream over the chocolate and stir gently until smooth and then set aside.

In a bowl using an electric hand mixer, or with a stand mixer fitted with the paddle attachment, beat the cream cheese until fluffy, scraping the sides of the bowl often. While beating, slowly pour in the sugar, again scraping the bowl often. Beat in the cornstarch. By this time the filling should be looking a little more fluid. Slowly pour in the hazelnut liqueur and beat in the eggs, 1 at a time. Pour in the chocolate mixture and blend well. Scrape the filling into the pan with the crust and bake for 30 minutes. Without opening the oven door, turn off the oven and leave in the cheesecake for another 30 minutes. Remove, let cool to room temperature, then chill overnight.

To serve, remove cheesecake from pan. (The cheesecake should slide off easily from the pan's base.) Dust the top of the cheesecake with cocoa powder and decorate with hazelnuts. *Makes one 9-inch (2.5 L) cheesecake • Serves 12*

TASTE The instant coffee in this cheesecake really serves to heighten the chocolate. Many chocolate recipes call for coffee as an ingredient for this same reason, not necessarily for the taste of the coffee itself.

TECHNIQUE To toast hazelnuts, spread them on an ungreased baking sheet and toast for 12 minutes in a 350°F (180°C) oven. Once cooled, rub the hazelnuts either in a tea towel or in a colander to remove the skin. The hazelnuts will look tidier, and the skin can have a bitter taste once toasted so it's best to remove it. Use pre-ground hazelnuts for the crust, as a food processor cannot process it to a fine powder and may turn it into nut butter.

TALE Bringing a chocolate cheesecake to the table seems to garner more oohs and aahs than a regular cheesecake.

CHOCOLATE MOUSSE CAKE

I love a good mousse cake, even though this dessert requires a little investment of time. This is two layers of rich chocolate cake with a mousse filling in the center, and a chocolate ganache that just covers the top and hangs over the sides a little, just enough to make the cake look polished but not so much that it hides the mousse filling.

CAKE

1½ oz **semisweet chocolate, chopped** 45 g
¾ cup **hot, freshly brewed coffee** 190 mL
1½ cups **sugar** 375 mL
1¼ cups **all-purpose flour** 310 mL
¾ cup **regular cocoa powder (not Dutch process)** 190 mL
1 tsp **baking soda** 5 mL
½ tsp **baking powder** 2 mL
½ tsp **fine salt** 2 mL
1 **large egg**
1 **large egg white**
6 Tbsp **vegetable oil** 90 mL
¾ cup **buttermilk** 190 mL
1 tsp **vanilla extract** 5 mL

CHOCOLATE MOUSSE

6 oz **semisweet chocolate, chopped** 175 g
½ cup **2% milk, at room temperature** 125 mL
1¼ cups **whipping cream (35%)** 310 mL
1 Tbsp **sugar** 15 mL
pinch **fine salt**

CHOCOLATE GLAZE

6 oz **semisweet chocolate, chopped** 175 g
⅓ cup **unsalted butter, cut into pieces** 80 mL
1 Tbsp **golden corn syrup** 15 mL

Preheat the oven to 300°F (150°C). Grease and line the bottom and sides of a 9-inch (2.5 L) springform pan with parchment, then grease the paper.

For the cake, put the chocolate pieces in a bowl and pour freshly brewed coffee over the chocolate, gently stirring to melt. Set aside. Sift the sugar, flour, cocoa, baking soda, baking powder and salt and set aside. In a large bowl, beat the egg and egg white using an electric hand mixer (or stand mixer) on high speed for 1 minute. While beating, slowly add the oil, buttermilk and vanilla. Alternate adding portions of the flour mixture and the melted chocolate mixture and beat until combined. Pour the batter into the prepared pan and bake for 1 hour to 1 hour and 10 minutes, or until a tester inserted in the center of the cake comes out clean. Allow cake to cool for 20 minutes in the pan, then turn out to cool completely, removing the parchment after it cools.

[continued next page . . .]

For the mousse, melt the chocolate in a medium-sized bowl over a pot of barely simmering water, stirring constantly. Remove from the heat and whisk in milk. Let cool to room temperature. In a separate bowl, whip cream to soft peaks and stir in sugar and salt. Fold cream into chocolate in 2 additions.

To assemble the cake, slice the cake in half horizontally and place the bottom half in a parchment-lined 9-inch (2.5 L) springform pan (the pan will hold the mousse and cake in place as it sets). Spread all of the mousse over the cake half, and top with the second cake half. Chill for at least 3 hours.

For the chocolate glaze, place the chocolate, butter and corn syrup in a bowl over barely simmering water and stir gently until melted and glossy. Let cool 15 minutes, stirring occasionally (see Technique).

Carefully remove the outside ring of the springform pan from the cake, and peel away parchment paper. Pour the chocolate glaze over the top of the cake in the center, and gently coax the glaze to the sides with an offset spatula. Let the glaze just catch the edges of the cake and drip down a touch. Chill cake until ready to serve. *Makes one 9-inch (23 cm) cake • Serves 10 to 14*

TASTE This is an ideal birthday cake for the chocoholic in your family. The top of the cake is a perfect canvas for writing "happy birthday." For this I would melt white chocolate and use it in a piping bag as my ink.

TECHNIQUE Letting the chocolate glaze cool a little—but not too much—is important. The glaze will keep getting thicker as it sits, and for the glaze to cling to the cake in slow-moving drips over the side, it has to be cool enough that it doesn't run right down the sides of the cake, but not so set that you have to force it. If the glaze thickens ups too much before you get to glazing, just reheat it until it's the perfect consistency.

TALE While I always look for a deal when buying kitchen supplies, I never skimp when it comes to springform pans. A good springform pan has a secure latch and makes a solid seal at the edge of the pan, so that nothing leaks out.

LEMON SPICE LAYER CAKE

I love lemon and spice together. The combination is seasonless—it suits a festive holiday meal in winter, but is equally appropriate served outside in midsummer.

1 cup **unsalted butter, at room temperature** 250 mL

½ cup **light brown sugar, packed** 125 mL

½ cup **granulated sugar** 125 mL

2 **large eggs, at room temperature**

1 cup **fancy molasses** 250 mL

3 Tbsp **freshly grated ginger** 45 mL

1½ Tbsp **finely grated lemon zest** 23 mL

2½ cups **all-purpose flour** 375 mL

½ tsp **baking soda** 2 mL

½ tsp **fine salt** 2 mL

¾ tsp **ground cinnamon** 4 mL

¼ tsp **ground nutmeg** 1 mL

¼ tsp **ground allspice** 1 mL

¼ cup **2% milk** 60 mL

¼ cup **lemon juice** 60 mL

LEMON-MASCARPONE FROSTING

1 cup **whipping cream (35%)** 250 mL

1 cup **icing sugar, sifted** 250 mL

2 cups **good quality mascarpone, at room temperature** 500 mL

1 tsp **finely grated lemon zest** 5 mL

2 Tbsp **lemon juice** 30 mL

lemon zest curls, for garnish

For spice cake, preheat the oven to 325°F (160°C). Grease two 8-inch (1.2 L) round cake pans, line the bottoms with parchment, grease again and then flour, shaking out excess.

In a large bowl, beat the butter using an electric hand mixer until light and fluffy. Add the sugars and beat well again. Add the eggs, 1 at a time, beating well after each addition. Continue beating on high speed for 2 minutes (this adds structure for a light cake). Reduce the speed to medium and add the molasses, fresh ginger and lemon zest.

In a separate bowl, sift the flour, baking soda, salt, cinnamon, nutmeg and allspice. Add to the butter mixture and stir just until incorporated.

[continued next page . . .]

Stir in the milk and lemon juice, and scrape into prepared pans, tapping pans gently to remove large air bubbles. Bake for 50 to 60 minutes, testing by pressing the center of the cake—it should spring back when pressed. Allow the cakes to cool 30 minutes in the pan before inverting to cool completely on a wire rack.

For the filling, whip the cream and icing sugar to soft peaks. In a separate bowl, beat the mascarpone gently to soften (see Technique), and then stir in the lemon zest and juice. Fold the cream into the mascarpone mixture.

To assemble, spread one-quarter of the icing on one cake layer, then top with second cake layer. Spread remaining icing just over the top, running a butter knife or off-set spatula through the icing in circles to create swirls. Garnish with lemon zest curls. Chill until ready to serve. *Makes one 8-inch (20 cm) layer cake • Serves 12*

TASTE This cake is similar to gingerbread in taste and texture but is a little more tender and not quite as heavy. The fluffy lemon-mascarpone frosting keeps it light and airy.

TECHNIQUE When working with mascarpone, it is important to be gentle. You can beat mascarpone to soften it so that the cream folds in more easily, but you don't want to be too vigorous. Because of the high fat content, mascarpone can end up curdling a bit like overwhipped whipping cream.

TALE I made a version of this recipe for my wedding. I left the sides exposed so it didn't look like a traditional wedding cake, and I topped the tiers with baby pears, plums and champagne grapes. We had an October wedding, so this suited the season.

PUMPKIN CHIFFON PIE This is a creamy, fluffy pumpkin pie that ends an autumn meal in style.

PASTRY
6 Tbsp **unsalted butter** 90 mL
6 Tbsp **vegetable shortening** 90 mL
1½ cups **all-purpose flour** 375 mL
2 Tbsp **sugar** 30 mL
½ tsp **fine salt** 2 mL
4–5 Tbsp **ice water** 60–75 mL

PUMPKIN CHIFFON
2 tsp **gelatin powder** 10 mL
4 **large egg yolks**
1 cup **sugar** 250 mL
2 cups **pumpkin purée** 500 mL
2 Tbsp **brandy** 30 mL
1 tsp **cinnamon** 5 mL
½ tsp **ginger** 2 mL
¼ tsp **cloves** 1 mL
2 cups **whipping cream (35%)** 500 mL
1 Tbsp **vanilla extract** 15 mL

For the pastry, freeze the butter and shortening for 30 minutes. Combine the flour, sugar and salt in a large bowl. Using a box grater, grate the chilled butter and shortening into the flour. Toss this mixture with your fingers to coat the fats, breaking up lumps with your fingers as you go. The dough should be a rough, crumbly texture and take on a slight yellow tone. Add 3 Tbsp (45 mL) of the water, and mix with a spatula or wooden spoon to bring the dough together, adding a little more water if needed. Shape the dough into a disc and chill for an hour before rolling.

Preheat the oven to 375°F (190°C). On a lightly floured surface, roll out the dough into a circle just less than ¼-inch (6 mm) thick. Gently lift the dough and line a 9-inch (23 cm) pie plate. Trim the edges and cinch into a fluted pattern. Chill the dough in the pie plate for 15 minutes. Line the pastry with foil and weigh down with dried beans, rice or pie weights. Bake the pie shell for 20 minutes, then remove the weights and foil and bake 10 minutes more, or until the bottom center of the pie shell is dry. Cool completely before filling.

For the pumpkin chiffon, soften gelatin in 2 Tbsp (30 mL) cold water. In a metal bowl over a pot of simmering water, whisk the egg yolks and sugar plus 2 Tbsp (30 mL) water until the mixture doubles in volume and holds a ribbon when the whisk is lifted (about 5 minutes). Remove from the heat and stir in the gelatin. Place egg mixture in a stand mixer fitted with the whisk attachment or use electric beaters and beat until cooled, another 5 minutes. Fold in the pumpkin, brandy and spices and chill until cool but not set, about half an hour.

While it's chilling, whip the cream to soft peaks and add the vanilla. Fold into mousse in 2 additions and then scrape into cooled pie shell. Refrigerate the pie for at least 4 hours before serving. *Makes one 9-inch (23 cm) pie • Serves 6 to 8*

TASTE This pie embodies all that is good about a traditional pumpkin pie, but it is much more light and airy. To make it family-friendly, you can replace the brandy with water—it won't compromise the recipe. (Do not skip adding the water, though, as the liquid is essential; the egg mixture would otherwise be too thick to whisk.)

TECHNIQUE The pumpkin chiffon makes a great mousse on its own. Skip making the pie crust and spoon the chiffon into serving glasses. A sprinkle of lightly toasted pecans makes a nice garnish.

TALE As soon as we get the first frost, I start craving those fall flavors like apple and pumpkin. And with those cravings comes the desire for the spices that go with them: cinnamon, ginger and cloves. I think it has to do with closing all the windows to keep the cold out—I then feel I have to fill the house with the cozy smells of baking.

LEMON CHEESECAKE MOUSSE TARTS

Pretty and fluffy, a lemon dessert pleases just about everyone.

Prepare the crust dough and chill. On a lightly floured surface, roll out dough to just less than ¼-inch (6 mm) thick. Sprinkle eight 4-inch (10 cm) tart pans (with removable bottoms) lightly with flour and line with pastry and trim off the edges. Chill for an hour.

Preheat the oven to 350°F (180°C). Place tart shells on a baking sheet. Dock bottom of the pastry with a fork, line shells with foil and weigh down with dried beans, rice or pie weights. Bake for 15 minutes, then remove weights and bake for another 8 to 10 minutes, or until the center of the tart shells appear dry and the edges are lightly browned. Let cool while preparing the mousse.

For the mousse, whip the cream to soft peaks and chill. In a separate bowl beat the cream cheese until smooth and beat in the sugar and lemon zest, scraping down the sides of the bowl often. Beat in the lemon juice and vanilla. Fold in the whipped cream in 2 additions. Dollop the mousse (or pipe with a piping bag) into cooled shells. Garnish with fresh blueberries and chill until ready to serve. Gently remove the outside rings and bottoms of the tart pans before plating. *Makes eight 4-inch (10 cm) tarts*

1 recipe **crust dough (see Bumbleberry Galette recipe on page 192)**
1½ cups **whipping cream (35%)** 375 mL
12 oz **cream cheese, at room temperature** 375 g
⅔ cup **sugar** 160 mL
1 Tbsp **finely grated lemon zest** 15 mL
½ cup **lemon juice** 125 mL
dash **vanilla extract**
fresh blueberries, for garnish

TASTE I personally like lemon and blueberries together, but you could garnish these tarts with any fresh berry. You could also put the berries under the mousse filling, on top or on the side.

TECHNIQUE This crust dough is versatile indeed. It handles easily in the Bumbleberry Galette recipe, but also suits a simple, creamy tart such as this. Make a double batch of the dough and freeze half so that you always have it on hand. Thaw it in the fridge overnight or on the counter for 3 to 4 hours. Knead lightly to soften before rolling.

TALE I call this my "cheater cheesecake." The fluffy filling tastes just like cheesecake, but doesn't require any baking.

BANOFFEE PIE

This is a satisfying winter dessert to make—bananas are always in season. Imagine them under a *dulce de leche* filling, all in an almond tart shell. Have I got your mouth watering? Then you'd better get baking!

PASTRY
1¼ cups **all-purpose flour** 310 mL
1 cup **ground lightly toasted almonds** 250 mL
⅔ cup **sugar** 160 mL
zest of 1 **lemon**
¾ tsp **cinnamon** 4 mL
pinch **ground cloves**
⅔ cup **unsalted butter, cut into pieces and chilled** 160 mL
1 **large egg**
1 **large egg yolk**
1 Tbsp **brandy** 15 mL

FILLING
3 **bananas**
1 can **(9½ oz/300 mL) sweetened condensed milk**
3 Tbsp **light brown sugar, packed** 45 mL
2 Tbsp **whipping cream (35%)** 30 mL
1 Tbsp **rum** 15 mL
1 tsp **vanilla extract** 5 mL
2 Tbsp **unsalted butter** 30 mL

TOPPING
1 cup **whipping cream (35%)** 250 mL
2 Tbsp **sugar** 30 mL
chocolate shavings or cocoa powder, for garnish

For the pastry, blend together the flour, almonds, sugar, lemon zest and spices. Cut in the butter until the texture of coarse meal. In a small bowl stir together the whole egg, egg yolk and brandy, and blend into the dough until it just comes together. Shape the dough into a disc, wrap and chill for 2 hours.

Preheat the oven to 350°F (180°C). On a lightly floured surface, roll out dough to just a little thicker than ¼-inch (6 mm). Line a 9-inch (23 cm) tart pan with the pastry, trim off the edges and chill 15 minutes. Dock pastry with a fork and bake for 20 minutes, or until golden brown around the edges. Let cool to room temperature.

For the filling, slice the bananas ¼-inch (6 mm) thick and arrange in the bottom of tart shell. Stir together the condensed milk and brown sugar in a heavy-bottomed saucepan. Have ready the remaining filling ingredients. Whisking constantly over medium heat, cook the condensed milk until it thickens and becomes a rich brown color, about 8 to 10 minutes (see Technique). Remove from the heat and whisk in the whipping cream, rum, vanilla and butter.

Pour the mixture over the bananas in the tart and spread evenly. Chill for 30 minutes.

For the topping, whip the cream to soft peaks and add the sugar. Spread the whipped cream topping on top of the tart. Sprinkle with chocolate shavings or a dusting of cocoa powder for garnish if you wish.

Makes one 9-inch (23 cm) tart • Serves 8 to 10

TASTE *Dulce de leche* is another flavor we can be grateful to South America for, alongside chocolate, coffee, tomatoes, potatoes and chilies. The intense sweetness and dairy richness make it an indulgence to be enjoyed in moderation, but I'll admit it's rare for me to have just one slice of Banoffee pie.

TECHNIQUE Be sure to stir that condensed milk constantly as you are cooking it. I find I have best success when I toggle between a whisk and a silicone spatula. It'll be quite fluid at first over the heat, but then it thickens as it cooks.

TALE I can't take credit for inventing this sinful combination. My friend Courtney introduced me to this dessert when I visited her in London, England. It is a popular dessert there that has really found a big audience here.

BUMBLEBERRY GALETTE

A galette is simply a single-crust, free-form tart. You don't even need to own a pie plate to make this. It is rustic yet polished-looking at the same time.

PASTRY

2 cups **all-purpose flour** 500 mL

½ cup **sugar** 125 mL

½ tsp **finely grated lemon zest** 2 mL

¼ tsp **fine salt** 1 mL

1 cup **unsalted butter, cut into pieces and chilled** 250 mL

1 **large egg**

1 **large egg yolk**

FILLING

2 cups **sliced strawberries** 500 mL

2 cups **fresh raspberries** 500 mL

2 cups **fresh blueberries** 500 mL

1 cup **fresh blackberries** 250 mL

5 Tbsp **sugar** 75 mL

2 Tbsp **cornstarch** 30 mL

pinch **ground cinnamon**

TO FINISH

1 **large egg mixed with** 2 Tbsp (30 mL) **water, for brushing**

turbinado sugar, for sprinkling

For the crust, stir the flour, sugar, lemon zest and salt to combine. Cut in the butter until the texture of coarse meal (this can be done in a food processor, with an electric mixer, or by hand using a pastry blender or your fingers). Whisk the egg and the egg yolk together, then add to the flour mixture, blending just until dough comes together. Shape the dough into 2 discs and chill for at least an hour.

Preheat the oven to 375°F (190°C) and line a baking sheet with parchment paper. Toss all the berries with sugar, cornstarch and cinnamon in a large bowl and set aside. On a lightly floured surface, roll out 1 pastry disc into a circle about 12 inches (30 cm) in diameter. Slide the dough onto the prepared baking sheet and spoon half the berries into the center. Fold pastry over berries in 6 folds, one overlapping another (only a bit of the berries need be visible in the center of the galette). Brush the pastry with egg wash and sprinkle with turbinado sugar. Bake for 35 to 45 minutes, or until the crust is a rich brown and the filling is bubbling. Repeat with the other pastry disc and remaining berries. Cool for 30 minutes before slicing. *Makes two 9-inch (23 cm) galettes • Serves 10 to 12*

TASTE Of course, any mix of berries in season is appropriate. I prefer using fresh berries in this recipe as opposed to frozen. The pectins present in fresh fruit actually help keep the filling together, even though a bit of the berry juice leaks out a little.

TECHNIQUE The technique of folding a galette is in *not* having a technique. The dough is very forgiving, so whether the galette gets four folds or eight it will all look and bake just fine.

TALE A galette in its truest definition is actually a French buckwheat crêpe that usually has a savory filling such as ham and cheese. The folding is the only thing that is familiar about what we now know as a galette.

CHOCOLATE STRAWBERRY TRIFLE

Trifle has come back in fashion. There was about a ten-year spell where trifle stopped appearing on menus or in food magazines, but it is making a solid comeback.

VANILLA POUND CAKE
¾ cup **unsalted butter, at room temperature** 190 mL
1¼ cups **sugar, plus more for the pan** 310 mL
1 Tbsp **vanilla extract** 15 mL
3 **large eggs**
2¼ cups **pastry flour** 560 mL
1¼ tsp **fine salt** 6 mL
1 tsp **baking powder** 5 mL
½ cup **buttermilk** 125 mL

CHOCOLATE CREAM
4 cups **2% milk, divided** 1 L
5 oz **bittersweet chocolate, chopped** 150 g
4 **large egg yolks**
¼ cup **cornstarch** 60 mL
½ cup **sugar** 125 mL
1 tsp **vanilla extract** 5 mL
1 tub **(1 lb/500 g) mascarpone cheese**

ASSEMBLY
1 cup + 1 Tbsp **sugar, divided** 250 mL + 15 mL
2 tsp **vanilla extract** 10 mL
6 cups **sliced fresh strawberries** 1.5 L
1 cup **whipping cream (35%), whipped to soft peaks** 250 mL
grated chocolate, for garnish

For the cake, preheat the oven to 300°F (150°C). Grease an 11- x 17-inch (28 x 42 cm) rimmed jelly roll pan and sprinkle the bottom and sides with sugar, shaking out excess.

Beat the butter with sugar in a large bowl until fluffy. Add the vanilla. Add eggs 1 at a time, mixing well after each addition. In a separate bowl, sift the pastry flour with salt and baking powder. Stir in a portion of the flour to the butter mixture alternately with a portion of the buttermilk, starting and ending with the flour. Scrape the batter into the prepared pan, spread to level and bake for 55 to 65 minutes, or until a tester inserted in the center of the cake comes out clean. Let cake cool for 15 minutes in the pan, then turn out to cool completely.

For the chocolate cream, in a saucepan heat 3 cups (750 mL) of the milk until just below a simmer. Place the chopped chocolate in a bowl. In another bowl, whisk the remaining 1 cup (250 mL) milk, egg yolks and cornstarch. Whisk in the sugar only when the milk has finished heating.

Slowly pour the milk into the egg mixture, whisking constantly. Return the mixture to the pot, and whisk over medium heat until thick and glossy, about 5 minutes. Remove from the heat, stir in the vanilla and pour through a strainer over the chopped chocolate, stirring until the chocolate is melted.

Place plastic wrap directly on the surface of the custard and chill for 2 hours. After the custard is chilled, beat the mascarpone cheese to soften slightly and whisk into the custard.

To assemble the trifle, bring 1 cup (250 mL) sugar and 1 cup (250 mL) water up to a simmer and stir until sugar has dissolved. Remove from the heat, stir in the vanilla and bring to room temperature.

Slice cake into pieces about the size of ladyfingers (1 inch/2.5 cm wide) and line the bottom of a 12-cup (3 L) trifle bowl with a third of the cake. Brush with cooled syrup and top with a third of the chocolate cream. Sprinkle 2 cups (500 mL) of strawberries over. Top with cake and repeat process 2 times, ending with strawberries. Stir the remaining 1 Tbsp (30 mL) sugar into the whipped cream and dollop on top of trifle. Garnish with grated chocolate and chill until ready to serve. *Serves 8 to 10*

TASTE This truly is a fabulous dessert to make when strawberries are in season. The classic trifle combination of cake, custard and fruit is magical when it is this heavenly combination of vanilla cake, chocolate custard and ripe, ripe strawberries.

TECHNIQUE If you are short on time, you can always make more of a tiramisù version by skipping the pound cake and using store-bought ladyfingers instead.

TALE At our last holiday open house, I set up a "trifle buffet" as the dessert station. I had five different trifles on display. I've already been asked if I'll be making the same desserts this year. I think I've started a tradition.

[PRESERVES]

Preserving is an art that is making a comeback. Where I live, it is routine to make jams and jellies and exchange them with friends and family. I have friends that actually book a day off work in August to "put up" tomatoes, so they will have good, basic tomato sauce year-round.

It is vitally important to follow safe canning procedures when processing any preserves. For details on safe canning procedures, I always follow guidance from www.homecanning. ca (go to www.freshpreserving.com in the u.s.). This is the bible for home canning, and gives explicit and correct instructions on how to safely process ingredients at home. The method varies depending on the recipe, but consider the following before beginning your own preserving ritual:

1. Follow the recipe exactly—while it may be tempting to reduce the amount of sugar in a jam, it helps set the jam to the right consistency *and* acts as a preservative so that the jam can be stored for a period of time outside of the fridge. If you wish to alter the recipe then you should no longer consider the preserve shelf-stable, and it should be kept refrigerated or frozen.

2. Always use new lids for your jars. Jars can be reused but not lids, so buy new ones each time. Follow the instructions that come with the lids—many require warming (*not* boiling!) before being snapped onto the jars, and the screw-on part of the lid should only be fastened *gently*, not tightly.

3. As the hot contents of the jar cool down, it creates a vacuum seal. If you notice that a few jars don't seal fully, then refrigerate those jars immediately. If later you open a jar and the lid doesn't "pop" when you open it, or it comes off too easily, then do not consume it—throw it out.

While safety is paramount, preserving at home is a process to be enjoyed and appreciated. It is so gratifying to open a jar in January of something you made during peak harvest season.

CHILI SAUCE

Chili sauce is a Canadian staple. The condiment can be used on burgers and on chicken, stirred into vegetables or even double as a salsa.

12 cups **peeled and chopped fresh tomato** 3 L
3 cups **diced onion** 750 mL
2 cups **diced green pepper** 500 mL
2–6 **banana peppers, diced**
5 cloves **garlic, sliced**

2 cups **sugar** 500 mL
1 cup **plain white vinegar** 250 mL
2 Tbsp **fine salt** 30 mL
1 Tbsp **dill seeds** 15 mL
1 Tbsp **celery seeds** 15 mL

Place the tomatoes, onion, green pepper, banana peppers and garlic in a large pot and bring to a simmer over medium heat. Cook for 15 minutes, or until peppers are soft. Add the sugar, vinegar, salt and spices and continue to simmer until excess water has cooked away and mixture is a sauce consistency.

Ladle the chili sauce into jars following proper canning procedures, including boiling the filled jars (without submerging lids) for 15 minutes. Store chili sauce in a cool dark place. *Makes about 6 cups (1.5 L)*

TASTE Chili sauce typically has a sweetness to it that makes it almost like ketchup meets relish. When you have chili sauce on hand, you really only need mustard and you can consider yourself set.

TECHNIQUE It is worth repeating that www.homecanning.ca (or www.freshpreserving .com) is the best resource for home canning procedures. They even have a 1-800 number to call if you find yourself mid-process and unsure of what to do. A great tip to add here is that while jars can be washed in the dishwasher, they still need to be boiled before filling, not only for sanitization but also to hold the heat that is vital in creating a good seal as the jar and its contents cool and create a vacuum.

TALE Our good friends Mike and Tina make loads of great chili sauce and salsa using vegetables they've grown in their garden, and they are kind enough to share it with us.

HOT PEPPER JELLY
Hot pepper jelly is as popular as ever. While it is traditionally served with cream cheese on crackers, it is also nice brushed onto grilled fish or chicken.

For the Hot Pepper Essence, bring all of the ingredients along with 1¼ cups (310 mL) water up to a boil over medium-high heat in a large pot. Reduce heat to medium, cover and simmer for 15 minutes, or until peppers are soft. Remove from the heat and let stand, covered, for 15 minutes.

Strain through a fine strainer or through a colander lined with cheesecloth into a large bowl. (Watch for pepper fumes when you lift the lid!) Then put it through a strainer lined with a coffee filter to make the essence as clear as possible. Chill for a few hours to let any remaining sediment settle in the bottom of the bowl.

Strain one last time through a coffee filter, ladling the essence from the bowl and taking care not to disturb the sediments at the bottom. Measure 2 cups (500 mL) and place into a large pot. Heat until warm and stir in the sugar. Bring liquid to a full boil and stir constantly for 1 minute. Stir in the pectin and return to a boil, stirring for 1 minute. Stir in the food coloring, if using.

Remove the pot from the heat, and remove any foam from the surface with a spoon. Transfer the jelly into jars following proper canning procedures, leaving a ¼-inch (6 mm) space from the top of the jar. *Makes about 5 cups (1.25 L)*

HOT PEPPER ESSENCE
1¾ cups **white wine vinegar** 435 mL
3 sprigs **fresh rosemary**
2 cups **diced and seeded red bell peppers** 500 mL
1 cup **diced and seeded hot red chili peppers or jalapeño peppers** 250 mL

FOR THE JELLY
2 cups **Hot Pepper Essence** 500 mL
5 cups **sugar** 1.25 L
1 pouch **liquid pectin**
red food coloring (optional—see Technique)

TASTE The addition of rosemary is my only little twist to give the jelly a depth of flavor that matches well with cheese and with main courses.

TECHNIQUE Straining it three times will ensure the clearest jelly. The food coloring, while optional in the recipe, gives the hot pepper jelly its recognizable hue. If you eliminate it from the recipe the jelly will simply be clear (the peppers themselves do not impart color).

TALE Late August and early September yield peppers to excess, and the farmers at the markets want to sell them quickly. I can't bear to see the peppers not find a home, so I tend to buy far more than I can use up, warranting a jelly-making session.

BREAD & BUTTER PICKLES
Bread and butter pickles have a nice sweetness to them and are a little milder than dill pickles.

4 **English cucumbers, sliced**
1 **medium onion, sliced**
2 Tbsp **coarse salt** 30 mL
1 cup **sugar** 250 mL
½ cup **apple cider vinegar** 125 mL
2-inch piece **fresh ginger, peeled and sliced** 5 cm piece
4 **whole cloves**
4 **whole black peppercorns**
½ tsp **pickling spice (see Taste)** 2 mL
¼ tsp **ground allspice** 1 mL
4 **English cucumbers, sliced**
1 **onion, peeled and sliced**

Put the cucumbers and onion in a bowl. Combine the rest of the ingredients in a heavy-bottomed saucepan. Bring to boil, stirring until sugar dissolves. Pour over the cucumbers and onion. Place a plate on the cucumbers to keep them submerged in pickling liquid. Cover and refrigerate at least 8 hours or overnight.

Pickles can simply be transferred to jars and be stored refrigerated for up to 8 weeks. But to preserve them for a longer period of time, strain the pickles and bring the pickling liquid to a boil. Place the cucumber slices in sterilized jars and pour the boiling liquid over. Seal the jars and cool. *Makes about 6 cups (1.5 L)*

TASTE Pickling spice can be found at the grocery store sometimes with the other spices, and sometimes with the canning jars and lids. It typically has bay leaf, mustard seeds, cloves, allspice, dill seeds, coriander seeds and even cinnamon.

TECHNIQUE This is a nice, small recipe that can be made and simply stored in the fridge. If you are canning these, however, it is important not to boil the jars of cucumbers. A cooked cucumber makes for a soggy pickle.

TALE If pickling cucumbers are available, they make for nice, small-sized pickle. Look for them throughout the summer at farmers' markets.

GARLIC PICKLED PEPPERS

This is a nice, small recipe that doesn't involve the whole canning procedure, in case making 36 jars of pickled peppers isn't your thing.

4 cups **thick wedges of red or yellow peppers** 1 L
1½ cups **plain white vinegar** 375 mL
½ cup **sugar** 125 mL
1 **medium onion, sliced**

8 cloves **garlic (kept whole)**
1 Tbsp **whole mustard seeds** 15 mL
1 Tbsp **fine salt** 15 mL
6 **whole black peppercorns**

Place pepper wedges in a two 4-cup (1 L) jars. Heat remaining ingredients plus 1 cup (250 mL) water to a boil and pour over the peppers. Allow to cool, then chill.

Store pickles refrigerated. *Makes 4 cups (1 L)*

TASTE Pickled peppers can be mild or hot—the choice is yours. Shepherd peppers make for mild pickles, while jalapeños can make for spicy pickles.

TECHNIQUE I wish I had some magic trick to tell how hot a jalapeño pepper is by looking at it, but there is no trick to judging them other than by tasting. The seeds do hold more of the *capsaicin* (the heat within the pepper), so if you want to make sure there is heat, leave a few seeds in the pickling brine.

TALE I like to use the pickled garlic cloves in this recipe chopped up in salad dressing—it adds a great, unexpected kick.

PLUM CONSERVE
This conserve can be used in place of cranberry sauce beside roasted turkey or pork. It is sweet but not too sweet, so you can also spread it on your toast in the morning.

Pit the plums and chop coarsely. Cut the orange in quarters and remove the seeds, keeping the peel on. Pulse in a food processor to chop finely. Place all the ingredients into a large, heavy-bottomed saucepan and bring up to a simmer over medium heat, stirring occasionally. Adjust the heat and simmer until conserve has thickened to a sauce consistency, about 15 to 20 minutes.

Pack conserve into sterilized jars and seal. Alternately, conserve can be packed into plastic tubs or resealable bags and frozen. *Makes about 9 cups (2.25 L)*

36 **Italian prune plums**
1 **large orange**
2 cups **sugar** 500 mL
¾ cup **dark brown sugar, packed** 190 mL
3 Tbsp **lemon juice** 45 mL
1 tsp **ground cinnamon** 5 mL
¼ tsp **ground cloves** 1 mL

TASTE By using the whole orange in this recipe, you get a marmalade-like edge from the peel, but still the gentle flavor of the juice within the orange.

TECHNIQUE I strongly favor the Italian prune plums over regular red plums. These prune plums are meant for cooking and baking, and make for an intensely "plummy" conserve.

TALE This recipe comes from my mom and is a great memory trigger for me. Growing up we had a plum tree in our backyard, and I remember helping my mom pit the plums for this conserve. It was a family favorite served beside my mom's pork roast.

MANGO CHUTNEY
I like to serve mango chutney alongside spicy foods to temper the heat of chili. Its sweetness balances dishes like the fragrant Samosa Sandwiches (on page 44).

2 cups **diced mango** 500 mL
½ cup **diced onion** 125 mL
⅓ cup **raisins** 80 mL
½ cup **light brown sugar, packed** 125 mL
3 Tbsp **plain white vinegar** 45 mL

1 Tbsp **finely grated fresh ginger** 15 mL
1 tsp **ground cumin** 5 mL
½ tsp **ground cinnamon** 2 mL
½ tsp **celery salt** 2 mL
3 Tbsp **finely chopped fresh mint (optional)** 45 mL

Combine all the ingredients except for the mint in a saucepan, and bring to a simmer over medium heat. Lower the heat and continue to simmer until the onions are tender and liquid has evaporated, about 10 minutes. Remove from the heat, and stir in the mint, if using. Pack into sterilized jars and seal, or simply cool and then chill until ready to serve. *Makes about 2 cups (500 mL)*

TASTE While you might expect mango chutney beside a curried dish, it also suits anything grilled, especially chicken or fish. I also use it as a condiment for burgers.

TECHNIQUE When peaches are in season, I replace the mango with the same measure of peeled and diced fresh peaches.

TALE Some people collect figurines, some people collect seashells. I collect condiments! The door of my refrigerator is packed with sauces and spreads, some homemade and some store-bought. I'm always looking for new and original flavor pairings, and I have noticed a surge in popularity of Indian spice blends and condiments.

SWEET PEAR CHUTNEY Like the Plum Conserve (page 203), this is a lovely companion to any roast.

Peel, core and dice the pears, tossing with the lemon juice. Add the pears (and their juice), sugar, lemon zest and cinnamon to a large, heavy-bottomed saucepan and bring to a simmer over medium heat. Cook uncovered, stirring occasionally, until pears are tender, about 20 minutes. Pack into sterilized jars and seal, or pack into tubs and freeze.
Makes about 8 cups (2 L)

12 **Bartlett pears, ripe but still firm**
3 Tbsp **lemon juice** 45 mL
2 cups **sugar** 500 mL
1 Tbsp **finely grated lemon zest** 15 mL
1 tsp **ground cinnamon** 5 mL

TASTE This is a sweet chutney making it quite versatile. In addition to serving beside a roast, it is delicate enough to be served over ice cream, beside gingerbread or stirred into plain yogurt.

TECHNIQUE Typically a chutney has onions and more of a savory edge to it. To make this into a more traditional chutney, you can add 1 cup (250 mL) finely diced onion and ⅓ cup (80 mL) raisins. I've presented the version above since it was my mom's recipe.

TALE Right after I would help my mom make her plum conserve, we switched right into pear chutney since we had two pear trees right next to the plum tree in our backyard. I think I preferred helping my mom with the plums because they were less work—plums don't have to be peeled!

BERRY LIME JAM
Lime is the unexpected twist in what is fundamentally a simple jam.

In a large pot, bring the berries to a simmer over medium-low heat, mashing roughly with a potato masher or flat spoon. Stir in the sugar and lime zest and juice, and cook for 2 minutes after it returns to a simmer. Add the butter, if using, and bring to a vigorous boil, stirring often, and cook for 15 to 20 minutes, periodically measuring the viscosity of the jam by dabbing a spoonful onto a plate and tipping the plate. Once the jam slows its drip down the plate (it should no longer run like a syrup), remove from heat and skim off foam.

Pack the jam into sterilized jars and seal. *Makes about 10 cups (2.5 L)*

8 cups **fresh, ripe straw-berries, hulled** 2 L

4 cups **fresh, ripe rasp-berries** 1 L

6 cups **sugar** 1.5 L

2 Tbsp **finely grated lime zest** 30 mL

½ cup **lime juice** 125 mL

1 Tbsp **unsalted butter (optional)** 15 mL

TASTE I like strawberry jam, and I *love* raspberry jam—but the quantity of seeds in raspberry jam can sometimes be excessive. By blending the two berries I get the best of both worlds.

TECHNIQUE This is a jam not set with added pectin, so while it will thicken a bit as it cooks down because of the pectin present in the seeds of the berries, it will never set like a traditional jam. This is more of a "spread" than a jam, meaning you can reduce the amount of sugar and it won't affect the end result.

TALE I also like to make this recipe substituting blueberries. I first cook two-thirds of the blueberries with the other ingredients, then purée the mixture and boil in the remaining one-third.

HOLIDAY FRUIT PRESERVE

This is a lovely preserve to have on hand at holiday time. The red cranberries and raspberries, subtle pear, spices and, of course, orange liqueur make it a festive treat to have on toast, bagels or croissants. This would make an ideal gift from your kitchen, perfect for a host gift or stocking stuffer.

4 cups **peeled and diced ripe Bartlett pears** 1 L

3 cups **fresh or frozen cranberries** 750 mL

2 cups **fresh or frozen raspberries** 500 mL

2½ cups **sugar** 625 mL

⅔ cup **orange juice** 160 mL

1 Tbsp **finely grated orange zest** 15 mL

1 tsp **ground ginger** 5 mL

½ tsp **ground cinnamon** 2 mL

¼ tsp **ground nutmeg** 1 mL

¼ tsp **ground allspice** 1 mL

¼ tsp **ground cloves** 1 mL

4 Tbsp **orange liqueur** 60 mL

Bring all the ingredients, except for the orange liqueur, to a simmer in a large, heavy-bottomed pot, stirring often. Simmer for about 15 minutes, or until pears are tender and cranberries have popped. Stir in the orange liqueur. Pack into sterilized jars and seal, or store refrigerated for up to 4 weeks. Holiday Fruit Preserve can also be frozen for up to 3 months. *Makes about 6 cups (1.5 L)*

TASTE Pears make up the base of this preserve, but they are so mild and subdued that they really act as a foil to the berries and spices.

TECHNIQUE The natural pectin in the cranberries does magic here to set a consistency to the preserve like a jam, simplifying the whole process.

TALE The truth is I sell a brand of holiday preserve at my store—I'm amazed how popular it is. I based this recipe on this product so that people could make it at home (but of course . . . I don't want to cut into my sales at the store!).

SPICED APPLE BUTTER
Apple butter takes the inherent goodness of apples and concentrates it by slow cooking.

Peel, core and dice apples and add to a large, heavy-bottomed pot along with the cider. Bring to a simmer over medium heat, then lower the heat and continue to simmer, stirring occasionally until the apples are tender, about 20 minutes. Purée in a food processor (or with an immersion blender). Return the apples to the pot, add the spices and simmer uncovered over medium-low heat for about 40 minutes, stirring often (see Technique). Add the honey and simmer, again stirring often, about 15 minutes more or until thickened—when lifting spoonfuls, it should mound a little. Pack the apple butter into sterilized jars, seal and boil for 10 minutes in a canning pot (without submerging the seals). *Makes about 6 cups (1.5 L)*

4 lb **McIntosh apples** 1.8 kg
1 cup **apple cider** 250 mL
3 **cinnamon sticks**
1-inch piece **fresh ginger** 2.5 cm piece
½ tsp **ground nutmeg** 2 mL
¼ tsp **ground allspice** 1 mL
¼ cup **honey** 60 mL

TASTE Apple butter is a lot smoother than applesauce because all the liquid is cooked away. Don't worry when the apple butter starts to turn darker than applesauce—it is part of the process. The natural sugars in the apples actually caramelize a little, giving the apple butter almost a toffee-apple taste.

TECHNIQUE McIntosh apples are my preferred apple for apple butter. They cook down to mush so quickly, which I don't like in my apple pie but is perfect for a smoothly textured apple butter. As the apple butter gets thicker and thicker and starts to caramelize toward the end of cooking, you will have to stir it more and more often so that it doesn't stick to the bottom.

TALE Because apple butter, unlike jam, has no added sugar (well, just a touch of honey), I don't mind slathering excess amounts on my toast in the morning.

[MENU BUILDING]

I have chosen to arrange this book in a more traditional format, arranging my dishes according to their category, or as you might find them listed on a restaurant menu.

Menu planning is a skill distinct from recipe writing, and while we do it every day, I'd like to share with you some suggestions for mixing and matching my recipes to build complete meals.

SIMPLE MEALS

Pappardelle Pasta with Squash, Ricotta & Sage (page 131)
Spinach, Beet & Orange Salad (page 25)

New York Strip Loin with Béarnaise (page 110)
Frites (page 126)

Bistro Skate Wing with Capers & Brown Butter (page 79)
Tomato Bruschetta Quinoa (page 133)

Arugula with Avocado, Blackberry & Feta (page 22)
Chicken Pot Pie (page 92)

Turkey Saltimbocca Pinwheels (page 101)
Lemon Melon Seed Pasta with Asparagus & Chèvre (page 132)

Vegetable Tagine (page 139)
Three-Onion Couscous (page 130)

PACK-A-LUNCH

SCHOOL
Ham & Herbed Cream Cheese on Raisin Bread (page 38)
veggie sticks
Chewy Oatmeal Nuggets (page 175)

OFFICE
Chickpea Pepper Toss (page 145)
Best Banana Bran Muffins (page 158)
Balance Cookies (page 178)

WEEKDAY SUPPERS

WINTER
Baja Fish Tacos (page 75)
Citrus Coriander Rice (page 127)
Bloody Caesar Tomatoes (page 150)

SPRING
Sesame Salmon with Roasted Red Pepper Salsa (page 86)
Three-Onion Couscous (page 130)
Berry Lime Jam (page 207) served over ice cream

SUMMER
Contemporary Cobb Salad (page 26)
Perfect Iced Tea (page 168)
fresh fruit

AUTUMN
Deconstructed Waldorf Salad (page 29)
Rockwell Bake (page 96)
Chewy Oatmeal Nuggets (page 175)

WEEKEND BRUNCH

Spiced Iced Coffee (page 167)
Cranberry Orange Scones (page 156)
Berry Lime Jam (page 207)
Asparagus & Chive Omelette (page 57) with Bloody Caesar Tomatoes (page 150)
Bumbleberry Galette (page 192)

HORS D'OEUVRE RECEPTION

Artichoke Asiago Squares (page 56)
Vietnamese Shrimp Salad Rolls with Peanut Dipping Sauce (page 62)
Easy Brandied Pork Terrine with Cranberry (page 64)
Mushroom Potato Brie Tarts (page 60)
cheese board with Plum Conserve (page 203) and Sweet Pear Chutney (page 206)

ENTERTAINING SUPPERS

WINTER
Shrimp Bisque (page 16)
Coq au Vin (page 91)
Lemon Spice Layer Cake (page 185)

SPRING
Roasted Leg of Lamb with Spring Herb Stuffing (page 118)
Lemon Melon Seed Pasta with Asparagus & Chèvre (page 132)
Lemon Cheesecake Mousse Tarts (page 188)

SUMMER
Asian Grilled Beef Flank Steak (page 109)
Spinach, Corn & Herb Stuffed Peppers (page 143)
Lemon Pesto Grilled Summer Vegetables (page 141)
Bumbleberry Galette (page 192)

AUTUMN
Garlic Roasted Turkey Crown with Chardonnay Pan Sauce (page 102)
Mascarpone Rough-Mashed Potatoes (page 125)
Moroccan Spiced Parsnips (page 148)
Parker House Rolls (page 155)
Pumpkin Chiffon Pie (page 187)

INDEX